HOODOO FOR LOVE AND PROSPERITY

AUTHENTIC ROOTWORK & CONJURE MAGIC SPELLS FOR LOVE, FRIENDSHIP, MONEY, AND SUCCESS

ANGELIE BELARD

HENTOPAN
PUBLISHING

© Copyright 2021 Angelie Belard - All rights reserved.

The content contained within this book may not be reproduced, duplicated, or transmitted without direct written permission from the author or the publisher.

Under no circumstances will any blame or legal responsibility be held against the publisher, or author, for any damages, reparation, or monetary loss due to the information contained within this book. Either directly or indirectly.

Legal Notice:

This book is copyright protected. This book is only for personal use. You cannot amend, distribute, sell, use, quote or paraphrase any part, or the content within this book, without the consent of the author or publisher.

Disclaimer Notice:

Please note the information contained within this document is for educational and entertainment purposes only. All effort has been executed to present accurate, up to date, and reliable, complete information. No warranties of any kind are declared or implied. Readers acknowledge that the author is not engaging in the rendering of legal, financial, medical or professional advice. The content within this book has been derived from various sources. Please consult a licensed professional before attempting any techniques outlined in this book.

By reading this document, the reader agrees that under no circumstances is the author responsible for any losses, direct or indirect, which are incurred as a result of the use of the information contained within this document, including, but not limited to, — errors, omissions, or inaccuracies.

CONTENTS

Introduction   7

1. An Introduction to Hoodoo   11
2. Preparation   23
3. Types of Workings   29
4. Spells for Love and Friendship   35
5. Spells for Money and Success   85

Conclusion   131

SPECIAL OFFER FROM HENTOPAN PUBLISHING

Get this additional book free just for joining the Hentopan Launch Squad.

Hundreds of others are already enjoying early access to all of our current and future books, 100% free.

If you want insider access, plus this free book, all you have to do is scan the code below with your phone!

INTRODUCTION

I have been a Hoodoo root worker for most of my life, and in my little corner of the world, I am respected for what I do. People travel to meet me to cast spells and create items that will aid them in their quest for success, friendship, love, and other life issues. I have done more workings than I can count, and I know that I have fewer years in front of me than I do behind me. As the years pass, I feel more and more strongly the urge to ensure that what I know about Hoodoo isn't lost.

My first book, *Hoodoo for Beginners*, was meant to teach the basics about Hoodoo. What it is and what it isn't, where it came from, and how it works. I'm proud of that book, but there is so much more to teach. Hoodoo has a history hundreds of years old, and it can't be taught in just one book.

In this book, I want to teach by doing. I know most people want a book of spells they can cast, but it's important to me that you know why the spells work the way they do. Which root is good in which circumstance, how to use candles, how to make your own conjure oils, mojo bags, spiritual baths and washes. And, most importantly, how to work with your ancestors, because they are the key to Hoodoo.

Don't worry, though, this book does have many spells (in Hoodoo we call them workings or conjures, but I'll bend with the tide on this one). Each spell has one key ingredient that I discuss, so you learn how it fits into Hoodoo. After you've read this book, it is my sincere hope that you will be able to make your own Hoodoo.

Some of the more common spells that people come to me for are love spells or money spells. With love work, they either want to draw love to them, to draw the right person, or to restore passion and commitment to a relationship. With money, people want more of it, or they desire success in business. These are fundamental human needs. The desire to love and be loved is strong and powerful. As humans, we were created to love and we also share the need to provide for those we love. Sadly, these needs are not always met. But it doesn't mean you should resign yourself to your fate. A simple spell can turn things around and you don't have to travel to see me for that. In this book, I share detailed spells designed for different purposes, but all are suitable for manifesting your desires for love and success.

Over the years I've used many of these spells, and many like them, for a client who has become a dear friend. To protect her privacy, I'll call her Maxine. I first met her when I was 27. She was a few years older than me, but we were kindred spirits. She had been through a very rocky patch in life and had just come out of a long relationship that had left her broken, broke, and completely battered.

Her first wish was to sever ties with this man because, on some level, she knew he was not good for her, but she kept going back. So, our first spell together was to break soul ties. After this was complete, she spent a year or two as a single woman, until she decided that she was ready for a new relationship. But things didn't go quite the way she hoped, as men didn't seem to notice her. We cast another spell together, this one to draw love to her. Within a few months, she had all the attention she'd ever dreamed of.

After a while, however, she realized what she really wanted wasn't an abundance of suitors, but rather, that one man who was right for her. As she reflected on her previous bad relationship, she realized she didn't want to waste time with someone who would turn out to be wrong for her. With the help of her ancestors, we designed a working to find the right man for her. A few months later, she met a wealthy widower! He was kind and caring. They connected. It was strong, it was beautiful, and it was passionate.

About a year or so later Maxine came back to see me. She told me that the relationship was great, but she wanted to move on towards marriage, and he seemed reluctant. She thought the loss of his first wife was holding him back, because he was afraid of becoming attached and then losing her. We created a spell to help him see clearly and to cast off his fear. Two days after we did the spell, he proposed. They got married and are still married to this day. Later, when Maxine decided to open her own beauty shop, we did several workings to guarantee her success, which she was, until she sold the business a few years ago.

I mention Maxine's story so you'll understand ahead of time that there's no "one spell" that will fix your life. Your circumstances and needs will change over the years, so if you can learn the "why" of the spell materials in this book, you'll be able to create your own successful workings. I have helped many people with Hoodoo throughout my life, but not everyone can come to see me in person, so I wrote this book because I want to help everyone use Hoodoo to improve their life.

The spells in this book are simple; there is nothing that requires the aid of an elder like myself. Even as a novice or beginner, you can search through the contents of your kitchen cabinets and gather the ingredients you need to create a spell so strong that it creates a doorway for those dreams of love and success to become your reality.

1

AN INTRODUCTION TO HOODOO

Before you can start using Hoodoo, you need to understand what it is, where it came from, and how it works. I covered this in *Hoodoo for Beginners*, so if you've read that book, feel free to skip ahead to Chapter Four, where the spells start. But if you haven't, I strongly encourage you to read the first three chapters of this book so you will have a solid, if introductory, understanding of Hoodoo.

Without understanding Hoodoo, trying to use the spells will get you nowhere. Hoodoo is a system, not a cookbook. You need to know the "why" before you learn the "how", so that you're not just going through the motions, and so that, eventually, you can create your own Hoodoo conjure.

We'll start with a short explanation of Hoodoo and its history, which will go a long way towards explaining the "why". I'll also share a bit of my own story, so you can understand how Hoodoo has affected my own life and the lives of those around me, and hopefully you'll see how it can affect yours in the same way.

A BRIEF HISTORY OF HOODOO

Hoodoo evolved from traditional African religions brought to the New World by enslaved Africans. The slave owners taught them a new language, dressed them in new clothes, gave them new food to eat, and attempted to "reform" them. Although they were separated from the people and everything they knew, some things were too deeply woven into their very existence to be altered or changed.

Slaves in the New World came from many areas of Africa, but frightened, confused, and abused in a strange land, they sought each other's company, finding comfort there. Gradually, they became a community, in which they shared their customs. The old ways of doing things that they'd brought with them were adjusted, tweaked, and manipulated to match their present circumstances.

Many aspects of Christianity were familiar to the African slaves. They already believed in one creator God, who was helped by powerful spirits to run the world, which they recognized in the Christian saints. They understood the Bible as a powerful spell book, and Hoodoo practitioners still use Bible verses in their work. In other words, Hoodoo is, historically, strongly based in Christianity. My grandmother Estelle, who taught me Hoodoo, was a devout Baptist, and met many of her clients after church on Sunday. We don't see Hoodoo as a separate religion or as being in any way in conflict with Christianity.

The African slaves incorporated more than just Christianity into their spiritual practices. They met Native Americans who helped them learn the power of the herbs and roots in this strange new land, and they incorporated aspects of European witchcraft and hex work. The slaves couldn't be picky about their tools, and the Hoodoo they did often involved life or death situations. If something didn't work, it just wasn't used. If you learn one thing from this book, I want it to be that **Hoodoo is practical**. If something works, use it. If it doesn't, discard it. You'll never see a Hoodoo spell that calls for Pink Himalayan Sea Salt, because slaves didn't have access to that kind of thing. But if there is a spell that calls for salt, and all you have is Pink Himalayan Sea Salt, then by all means use it!

The African religions evolved differently depending on where the slaves landed in the New World. In the larger Catholic plantations of Cuba, for instance, the slave owners had less direct control over the slaves, so they were better able to maintain their traditional practices. Those slaves focused more on the Catholic saints as being aspects of spirits from their homeland, and their practices grew into Santeria. In Haiti, also strongly Catholic, the practices grew into Voodoo, which played a large part in the revolution that freed the island's slaves from the French. In other places, the African religions developed into practices like Candomblé, which was practiced in Brazil.

On mainland North America, there were fewer slaves per slave owner, so the slave owners had more control, which made it harder for the slaves to practice their traditional spiritual ways. Hoodoo evolved in those mainland colonies, which is why Hoodoo is less of an organized religion compared to Voodoo or even Santeria. You don't need to be initiated into Hoodoo, and there's no hierarchy among practitioners. You'll also find that Hoodoo differs from place to place.

HOODOO BELIEFS

Let's talk about exactly what Hoodoo is in practical terms. It shares many qualities with practices like Voodoo and European-based witchcraft, so it's important to know what is different about Hoodoo.

Ancestral Veneration

I think working with the spirits of our ancestors is, perhaps, the key part of Hoodoo that separates it from other spiritual and magical practices. The spirits of your ancestors can be called on for aid and guidance. It's important to develop a relationship with your ancestors, and not simply call on them when you're in need, like a fair weather friend who you only hear from when they need something from you. How long would you stay friends with someone like that? Everyone practicing Hoodoo must have an ancestor altar, and I'll explain more about what that means in Chapter Two.

Rootwork

There is power in roots and herbs, and you can call on that power. In Hoodoo, we call this rootwork, and you'll find roots and herbs in nearly every Hoodoo spell. You can usually understand why an herb is used by understanding the plant it came from, the aspects of the herb itself, or the effects it has on the human body. For instance, cinnamon is a common herb used to speed up drawing work, because cinnamon is both sweet and a bit warm to the tongue. The sweetness will draw things to it, just like a bear being drawn to honey. And the heat will make the work faster, just like in cooking or chemistry.

Sometimes the "why" of a root is biblical. For instance, hyssop is used in purification and cleansing because it is mentioned as being used in the Bible (Psalm 51:7 "Purge me with hyssop, and I shall be clean"), and the Bible is understood to be a powerful spell book.

Devil's Shoestring is often used to "trip up the devil", which in Hoodoo means to keep evil away or end bad habits. Our ancestors knew how to use it because the roots of this plant are a twisted mess and are great at causing things to lose their footing.

Not everything we call rootwork is a root or herb, though. We'll use items like keys for opening new possibilities, or dice for luck, or money for prosperity.

The Power of the Earth

Just as roots and herbs have power, so does the earth itself. The energy around some locations can seep into the dirt, and you can harness that energy by using that dirt. For instance, money flows into and around banks all day, so you can collect the dirt from outside a bank to use in money drawing work. Similarly, the dirt from a church is good for purification and cleansing, as well as helping to bring about marriage. Dirt from a hospital can be used for healing magic, dirt from near a court can be used for justice, and so on.

There are two special cases of using earth that I want to discuss in a bit more detail, and the first is graveyard dirt. Graveyard dirt is special because it can be used in a number of different ways, and also because collecting it is more involved than it is at other locations. Dirt in a graveyard hasn't just collected the energy of a place, it has also collected the energy of the spirits that reside in that graveyard. A graveyard is home to many spirits, like a neighborhood, and you should not enter such a place without showing respect. First, whenever you enter a graveyard, you should cover your head. This is both a sign of respect and a way to block the spirits from attaching themselves to your mind. Second, always bring with you an offering to leave at the entrance. This can take several forms, but the most common are rum, sweet bread, or three pennies.

After respectfully entering the graveyard, you'll also have to find a spirit whose grave you want to work with. The dirt from graves of different spirits has different effects. The dirt from a gambler's grave can be good for luck work, while the dirt from a murderer's grave is good for crossing. I strongly suggest that the first time you collect graveyard dirt, you do so from the grave of a loved one. And before ever collecting graveyard dirt, you must develop a relationship with the spirit of that grave. Introduce yourself as you would when entering someone's home. Make small talk and ask the spirit about itself. At first, you'll find it hard to hear what they have to say. It may manifest as the blowing wind, a feeling in your stomach, a tingling in your fingers, or just as sudden intuition. And speaking of intuition, always trust yours. If you have a bad feeling about a grave, stay away.

The second location you need to know more about when it comes to using its dirt is a crossroads. In Hoodoo, a crossroads is anywhere two roads meet to form an X. The importance of the crossroads descends from African traditions of the Congo, whose people knew that spirits reside at crossroads. These spirits have different names, but what is important to know is that, like at a graveyard, you must show respect to these spirits. Don't just go to a crossroads and collect the dirt! You have to first establish a relationship and show that you will give something in exchange for what you take. Like at a graveyard, offerings of sweets, rum, or coins will do. I tend to carry some butterscotch hard candies in my purse. The spirits like them, and so do I.

The crossroads is used for many things in Hoodoo, but usually it involves the idea of carrying something away. If you want to sever ties with a person, you can incorporate crossroads dirt into your work. If you need to dispose of the remnants of a spell, you can bury it at a crossroads so the energy will be cleanly dispersed.

HOODOO AND THE BIBLE

As I mentioned earlier, the history of Hoodoo and Christianity in America are intertwined. Our ancestors recognized the Bible as a powerful spell book, and most rootworkers in the past have viewed themselves as Christian. While I admit I haven't been to church as much as I should, my Bible is always open to one page or another. Readings from the Bible are incorporated into many Hoodoo workings, such as Isaiah 55:11 "So is my word that goes out from my mouth: It will not return to me empty but will accomplish what I desire and achieve the purpose for which I sent," which is good for any reading during any working, if you can't find something more specific.

With that said, you do not have to be a Christian to work Hoodoo. Our ancestors worked magic long before they came to this land, and so can you. For some of the spells in this book I'll mention Bible readings that are appropriate, but consider them optional. If you don't use them, it's always good to explain to your ancestors what you want to accomplish. No matter what your beliefs, your ancestors will aid you.

MY HOODOO HISTORY

While Hoodoo has been around me all my life, I never set out to be a conjurer. I was familiar with our ways of doing things thanks to my mother and my father. Neither of them was a typical Hoodoo practitioner, in the sense that they rarely sat down to make up spells for specific purposes. However, they possessed certain eccentricities that made it clear to others that they were connected to our practice. My father, for instance, always went to bed with a herbal mojo bag under his pillow for protection. My mother regularly cleansed the house to clear out bad energy and ward off evil spirits. But my grandmother, Mama Estelle, was famous as a conjurer. People from all over Louisiana came to her for spells. Word of her legendary gifts spread so widely throughout our community that even in school, the boys were afraid to mess with me because there were rumors that she could put a hex on them. Of course, none of that was true. But her reputation was one of the factors that added to my positive experience in high school.

At the age of 13, I started apprenticing under Mama Estelle. Our intention wasn't for me to become a full-time conjurer. She simply felt that my parents weren't adequately carrying the tradition and that someone in the family needed to be given all the knowledge that she had accumulated over the years in order to pass it on to the next generation. When she died, there was a hole in my heart and my life. Through self-reflection, as well as some of the experiences I had at that time, I concluded that Hoodoo was that element I needed to fill up that empty space. It has been more than four decades since her passing and I have never looked back. I enjoy every moment of my life as a conjurer. I don't particularly like being called that, though. It's a name the people outside our community came up with. I am simply Angelie.

I practice Hoodoo because it is who I am. I love connecting with the power within as well as the powers that are around us. I am happiest when I create a spell and watch my dreams or expectations manifest. As you begin to practice, you will find that your connection to Hoodoo is not the same as mine. But it will give you fulfillment as it has given me. The spells in this book focus on love and financial success and I believe that this is something we all have a right to enjoy. Many people come to me with problems that have simple solutions that they could have created in their backyards. I feel it is my responsibility to pass on the knowledge of my ancestors to this generation and perhaps even the one after it.

HOODOO AS A WAY OF LIFE

You can't talk about Hoodoo from a native perspective without going into stories from the motherland. These stories were orally passed on to us by our ancestors. You will not find them on the pages of history books. Even in the books of those who have tried to chronicle our history for us, Hoodoo is not a religion or a belief. It is the way we live our lives.

Our ancestors lived off the land. This meant that when they were sick, it was the land that provided healing. If they needed love, they turned to the land. On the land is where they would find water, herbs, and any other accoutrements that, when combined, could provide solutions to the problems that plagued them. Courage, community, and culture inspired them at every level, and continue to inspire us.

What do I mean by courage, you may wonder? Courage to face problems head-on instead of running away from them. Courage to embrace every part of oneself even though it may not favorably tally up against the opinions of the public. Courage to do what is necessary to achieve the results you desire. This was the kind of courage my people spoke and sang about.

When it comes to community, our practice is a communal one. The energy that we tap into when creating spells is a powerful communal or ancestral energy. We feed on the energy of our past and bind it to our will/intention in the present.

Finally, we come to culture, which is our way of life. Hoodoo is not some secret cult practice that we hide in the back of our closet only to put on a mask to present when we are in public. It is the very essence of who we are. The more you incorporate Hoodoo into your day-to-day living, the more powerful your spells will become.

When we wake up in the morning, there are specific habits and rituals that we carry out to get our day started on the right note. These rituals provide protection and enhance our overall spiritual atmosphere. But this doesn't mean you have to automatically change the way you do everything. Hollywood has portrayed Hoodoo in a way that makes it difficult to picture us 'conjure folk' as normal people. But believe me, the Hoodoo culture is very regular. I believe we're simply more in touch with nature.

Most Hoodoo practitioners are very connected to the earth. You'll find us tending mini herbal gardens that not only serve a practical purpose in the kitchen but also provide easily accessible herbs that we can use to create tinctures and spells. When we take a bath, we don't just use soap and water to wash off the dirt of the day. We make it a spiritual experience by using herbs tied to specific intentions to attract what we want.

When you create spells after Hoodoo has already become a part of you, those spells will be more potent.

2

PREPARATION

Now that we have brushed up on what Hoodoo is, let us look at what goes into the preparation of a spell. You can't just waltz into your ancestral altar with the ingredients, say a few incantations, and hope for the best. There is a ritual that needs to be followed to guarantee the success of that spell and that will be our focus in this chapter.

ENERGY

Your energy plays a very important role in the spells that you cast and that energy is fed by your mind. If your mind is not in the right place, it can influence the outcome of your spell. This is why it's very important to work on your energy before you get into spell-casting. There are a couple of things we will talk about in each spell that we create that enable you to purify your energy and ensure that it remains positive. Think of your spells as a computer. The information you feed into it will be relayed back to you. When your energy is not focused, it creates discord or disharmony in the rhythm of the spell. This is something you may not pick up on as a beginner. But as you continue to practice, you can intuitively detect the mood of a spell and determine the mental state of the person who cast it.

So, before you set out to create a spell, you have to get into the right mindset. I like to take a walk in the woods near my home, which always brings me a sense of peace. I love gardening and humming in the garden while I work takes my mind off whatever is bothering me and puts me in a positive state. When I'm doing love drawing work, I like to listen to romantic music.

You will have to find what works for you, but at the end of the day, the objective remains the same. You want to set the tone for the spell that you are going to cast. For some people, it can be rigorous exercise or watching a few funny videos on YouTube. It could even doing a simple meditation exercise. Do whatever calms your mind and prepares it to create a spell.

People who cast love and prosperity spells are often doing so from a place of desperation. This is not positive energy. It will only give birth to an outcome that inspires the same feeling. If you desire success, you must mirror that successful attitude with your energy. If you want love, mirror those feelings with your energy.

YOUR ANCESTOR ALTAR

One of the most sacred aspects of Hoodoo practice is the space where you carry out your spell. Within our community, this space is commonly known as the ancestral altar. This is where you pay homage to the ancestors who paved the way for you, and then tap into their powers to create and manifest the desires of your heart. An altar is a place of transformation and the starting point of manifestation.

The altar is the space through which your ancestors can give their blessings and pour their power into the spells cast by you. It is where you will feel the most powerful. Your altar is crucial to your Hoodoo practice and is traditionally meant to be somewhere in your home. However, it is not uncommon to place it outside your home, in a location where you feel most connected to your ancestors.

Either way, your ancestral altar does not need to be in a glamorous location. The important thing is to use it to connect with the power of the people who came before us. Long ago, Hoodoo practitioners established this connection by adding items known to have a direct link to their forebears. For example, my grandmother Estelle gifted me the Bible of my great, great grandmother. Even if you don't have something like this, a picture of your ancestors would suffice, particularly if it is of those with whom you have fond memories.

Another thing that must be present in your altar or space where you cast a spell is a glass of water. This is an offering to your ancestors, and a kind of spiritual alarm bell. When something unusual is going on spiritually, it can often be seen by careful study of the water. If the water is evaporating faster than it should, or is bubbling in a strange way, it may be that your ancestors are trying to get your attention.

You should also leave your ancestors other offerings at your altar. If you knew your ancestors, offer them things they liked in life. If not, things like rum, or cigar smoke, or candies are usually well accepted.

INTENTIONS

When you create a spell, you summon powers and then you put those powers to work with your intentions. It is not enough to put the items together for all the rituals, speak some words, and hope for the best. You must be clear on the mission you want those powers to accomplish and clarity of mind is inspired by intention. Again, this is where binding your conjure or chore to a Bible verse makes a huge positive difference. When you know what you want in very explicit terms, you will make it easier for the arrow to find its target. This is especially important when you are creating a love spell. You can't just say you want someone to fall in love with you when you haven't determined what exactly you want to do when they actually fall in love with you. If you shoot an arrow under windy conditions, it will likely miss its mark because of the wind.

The same thing happens when you make a spell. It moves towards the objective but the world outside of the physical plane is very different. There are waves of forces moving at the same time. Always remember that one event can create multiple outcomes. Your spell needs to be heightened by your intention, so that those forces that may conflict with your objective will not be able to deter or slow down the potency of your spell. This way, when it reaches its target, the outcome is a satisfying one.

I had situations in which my clients carried out a love spell efficiently on their own but somehow got an undesirable result. The spell worked... just not in the way they had hoped. It is like cutting down a tree. You sharpen the axe blade, grab the handle, and then swing in the direction of the tree. Experienced tree cutters will tell you that you also need to pay attention to where you cut. If you don't, the tree could fall anywhere, including on top of you.

Your intentions anchor the spell and keep it on the path you want it to go. This way, when it accomplishes what it set out to do, it doesn't turn into an unpleasant experience. Another effective method of strengthening your intention is by strengthening your ancestral connection. Their spirits will not only fire up your spell, in a love spell, they will lead you to the right person for you. Know what you want. Be crystal clear about it. Rid your mind of thoughts that conflict with your desires. During conjuring, it is a good idea to use a candle to center your focus and thus sharpen your intention.

CLEANSING AND PURIFICATION

Before doing any Hoodoo, it's important to perform some kind of spiritual cleansing. Having a regular cleanse is the way of life for people who practice Hoodoo. For us, a cleanse is beyond washing off your body with soap and water. You have to purify yourself and this purification provides fortification.

When you tamper with powers beyond the physical plane, you expose yourself. With or without fortification, there are dark spirits that will ride on the waves of that ancestral connection and enter into your space. A thorough cleanse will ward off their impact and cause them to be powerless. But when you fail to do a cleanse, you will absorb that impact and as you continue to cast spells, they will begin to change form and become darker until the darkness consumes you. If the spell is intended to be a love spell, this darkness will also consume the person your spell is directed at.

My grandmother explained it to me this way: The powers of our ancestors are like the ocean. When you look at the ocean, you see water. But there are strong forces pushing and pulling the water in different directions. A cleansing bath puts a barrier on your body and allows you to swim in the ocean to your target and then return without having the ocean overwhelm you. The water will roll off your back and onto the floor without causing any damage.

In the chapters where I talk about the spells, I include an important cleansing ritual that you must carry out before you cast any spell. Even when you are not casting a spell, it is a good idea to take cleansing baths. Not only are they good for your skin, but they also keep your mind and body in a positive state. They offer an extra layer of protection and also help to maintain a positive aura.

3

TYPES OF WORKINGS

As I mentioned, in Hoodoo we don't usually call it a spell, but I know most people outside of Hoodoo use that word, so I'll use it in this book interchangeably with "working" or rootwork or conjure, which is what we do in Hoodoo. There are several types of work in Hoodoo you should be familiar with.

SPIRITUAL BATHS

A Hoodoo spiritual bath is a way of applying the power of rootwork directly to your skin, the closest kind of contact you can get. There are many types of spiritual baths, but the most common is performed as a spiritual cleansing. You can wipe away any negative energy or spirits, and even bad luck that may have become attached to you. This restores your spiritual balance, leaving you better able to perform Hoodoo workings, and to make those workings more powerful. Also, they can serve as a fortification ritual. If you are seeking to protect yourself from bad energy, bad vibes, or even bad spells; there are types of spiritual baths that give you an added layer of protection.

A spiritual bath can also be used to turn your body into a kind of magnet that attracts the things you desire. This is particularly useful when you are creating a love spell. They are also used to disengage the forces of a negative spell that has been cast over you. In other words, if you have been cursed, spiritual baths are one of the things you have to do to end the power of that curse over your life.

FLOOR WASHES

Just as a spiritual bath is used on the body, a Hoodoo floor wash can be used on your home or place of business. For example, if you move into a new space and you have some bad vibes or you feel the presence of an evil entity, a thorough floor wash can cleanse the energy in that space and build a boundary that will push back any negative vibes hovering around the home. You can also use a floor wash to set up barriers around the house or space so that certain types of energy, spirits or even people are unable to locate or enter that space. This protection barrier will have to be renewed consistently to keep it potent and effective.

Just like spiritual baths, a floor wash can also be used to create a field of attraction. This is particularly useful for businesses. You want to be able to attract the kind of clients that will boost your business profile and also attract wealth and opportunities to it. A floor wash works hand in hand with conjure oils and mojo bags.

MOJO BAGS

A mojo back, sometimes called a gris-gris, is a small pouch that contains rootwork made of herbs, oils, and other items. This creates a small spirit that you carry with you. This little spirit can be directed to help you achieve your aims, whether they be for love, luck, money, protection, or just about any kind of working. Mojo bags work like a power bank to support whatever intentions you have and can be formulated to suit any purpose.

I am a huge fan of mojo bags, because sometimes you may not always have the energy to concentrate your intentions and focus on the purpose of the spell you have created. For example, if a mojo bag was created for love and you happen to be in the place where you have potential candidates, a mojo bag will amplify the power of the spell you created earlier and set things in motion. If it was created for protection, you might find yourself in a situation that appears safe but is unknown to you, and there might be hidden elements that pose a threat to you. A mojo bag will detect this threat and activate the protective layer around you. In short, it is designed to be a portable power generator that ensures your spell stays powered up at all times.

The spirits of the mojo bags must be fed to stay active. You can generally feed a mojo bag smoke or rum, but sometimes you should feed it conjure oils or other things more appropriate to the spirit within. For instance, a mojo bag for luck might be fed Van Van oil, which is good for luck, while one for protection might be fed Florida Water.

CONJURE OILS

Conjure oils are oils that have been infused with the power of roots and herbs, and are useful when directly applying the roots or herbs can be problematic. For instance, it's easier to dress a candle with a conjure oil than it is to dress it with many different herbs.

Conjure oils are made by adding a blend of herbs to a carrier oil, like sunflower oil, and binding them to a purpose. They can be used to dress candles, as I mentioned, to feed mojo bags, in spiritual baths and floor washes, and in just about any Hoodoo work.

Let's say you wanted to create a love spell. Getting a conjure oil designed for love can help increase the potency of that spell. You can put it in your cleansing bath, use it in a floor wash, pour it into your mojo bag mix, or use it to bless the candle that you will be working with.

Conjure oils are created for specific purposes. It is important to understand that there is no conjure oil that works for everything. It has to be created for a specific purpose. When you are buying it from a Hoodoo practitioner, be sure that they know what they are doing because the potency is linked to the intentions and energy of the person who created it. If you buy from the wrong source, the outcome of your spell may not be satisfactory. On the bright side, conjure oils have a longer shelf life than mojo bags. They don't need to be reworked to maintain their potency. When you buy from a good source, it lasts as long as it is available.

ROOT WORK

Of course, at the heart of almost every Hoodoo spell is root work. Plants contain energy that you can use in your magic, and understanding what kind of energy they contain is the key to mastering Hoodoo. When you know how herbs interact with each other, you develop an inner system that allows you to bring these items together to serve you. You will harness the powers that lie dormant within them and use them to channel the power of your ancestors to bring to life the thing that you desire the most.

4

SPELLS FOR LOVE AND FRIENDSHIP

Love is a beautiful feeling. To love someone and have that person love you back in a way that is wholesome is something we all desire. I am 1000 percent in love with love. I love being in love. I love seeing people fall in love. But more than that, I love to see people going the distance together while in love. Have you ever watched a couple in their 80s or 90s celebrating love after spending more than half of their life with each other? It is pure and beautiful to behold. To find companionship that lasts you on the journey of life is something that most of us want. Sadly, not many of us can achieve that dream.

So, we turn to other means to guarantee our happily-ever-after. One way to welcome lasting love into your life is through a love conjure. But before you dash off to your altar, there is something you should know. Love spells do not make someone fall in love with you. They can draw love to you, make someone new notice you, and even remind someone of a time when they were in love with you in the past. But they will not force another person to fall in love with you.

As I've explained, Hoodoo derives its potency from our connection to our ancestral spirits. These spirits often act as guides. Because they see beyond the physical eye and operate in a different realm, they are able to pull your lover towards you.

My grandmother was fond of saying that there is a cover for every pot. This phrase is what she said to clients who came to her for love spells. For some reason, by the time these people came to my grandmother, they had all but given up on the idea of love. They had even convinced themselves that no one could love them. But she firmly shut them down with that little phrase, and then set to work with a love conjure that showed them how wrong they were.

All they needed was an open channel that draws their beloved closer to them faster. This is where your ancestral spirits come in. They help to locate this person who is uniquely suited for you. Then they forge a circumstance that bridges the distance between the both of you. Know this; your ancestral spirit will never bring someone who may cause harm to you. Nor will they force someone to love you against their will.

If you are having problems in your current relationship, a love spell can make your partner open to suggestions but they will never be manipulated to a point where they are no longer making decisions of their own free will. I have had clients come to me for love spells but when they finally meet someone, they start questioning the authenticity of the relationship because they worry the person is with them against their will. Hoodoo rootwork is nothing like that.

Another thing I should cover before we get into the love spells is your state of mind. I know you have been searching for love. You have probably been hurt by love and maybe even feel a little desperation to find love at all costs. You are going to have to leave all of those emotions outside your door. Feelings of desperation, loneliness, pain, hurt and betrayal do not create the right atmosphere within you for a love spell.

Before you cast the spell, you need to fall in love with the idea of love. One quick way for me is to play some Al Green music. Whatever type of love spell I'm working on, that man has a song for it. His words stir my heart.

You need to find a way to get to this point. Don't make it about the person you are hoping to meet or the spell you are trying to create. It is about activating an atmosphere of love inside of you so that you become the beacon that attracts the love you seek for yourself. This is perhaps one of the most crucial elements when creating a love conjure. Now, let's begin.

LOVE DRAWING OIL WITH ROSE PETALS

Conjure oils are one of the most commonly sold items in any Hoodoo shop, and Love Drawing Oil is probably any shop's best seller. You can use conjure oils in many other Hoodoo workings - in a mojo bag, to anoint a candle, or in spiritual washes and baths. You can also use it directly on your skin like a cologne or perfume. This Love Drawing

Oil can be used by both men and women. It is a beginner-friendly rootwork that is almost impossible to get wrong.

Before you can make this conjure oil, or any other, for that matter, you need to select a carrier oil. You want an oil that is malleable and easy to work with. Almond oil, sunflower oil, and rapeseed oil are my personal favorites, and I prefer almond oil for love work. In our community, there are a lot of varying opinions on which oil is the best. But one thing we all agree on is that whatever oil you use, it is better to go with a more natural oil than a synthetic one. Olive oil can also work as your carrier oil but I don't use this as a first option because it is very thick. I have friends who lighten the olive oil with natural essential oils. This can be a good option as well.

If none of the options I mentioned are immediately available to you, your good old-fashioned cooking oil will do just fine. If you learn one thing from this book, I hope it's that Hoodoo is adaptable and practical. Use what works.

This conjure oil features rose petals, a common ingredient in Hoodoo love workings. The sweet scent of a rose has been associated with love for thousands of years, so it probably comes as no surprise to find that it's used in Hoodoo. You can alter this oil to suit your needs by changing the color of the rose petals used, or mix and match to combine.

What You Will Need

- Carrier oil - five tablespoons
- Five rose petals (pink for romance, red for passion)

- Jasmine oil (to draw romance) - three drops
- Patchouli oil (to draw love) - three drops
- Dried orange peel (for purity) - a few pieces
- Strainer
- Bottle
- Mortar and pestle

The Work

1. Add the jasmine oil to the carrier oil. Swirl (do not shake) and set aside.
2. Manually blend the rose petals, dried orange peel, and patchouli in a mortar. Be careful not to turn the herbs into a paste! We want to do just a little more than bruise them to extract their essence.
3. Put the oils and herb mixture together and pour into the bottle, then store for seven days.
4. During those seven days, shake the bottle once a day.
5. Pour the mixture through a strainer into a clean bottle. The oil in the clear container is your Love Drawing Oil. You can discard the herbs, or store them away in a dry place to use in future love work.

This oil can be used in many ways. You can pour it on your candle before you light it for work. You can put a few drops in your bathwater or sprinkle it on your vision board or journal/list where you write down the things you want to manifest in your relationship. It can also be useful when preparing your mojo bag for love or friendship.

If you're a Christian, or looking for something to say as you make the Love Drawing Oil, you can pray with Psalm 63:1.

FINDING LOVE WITH HONEYSUCKLE

Honeysuckle is probably my favorite plant to teach people about Hoodoo with because it's useful for many things. If you have ever seen a honeysuckle vine, you might be able to guess why. The sweet-smelling flowers of the honeysuckle are perfect for drawing love. But the majority of a honeysuckle vine is covered with green leaves, not flowers, which is why the leaves of the honeysuckle are for drawing money and abundance. The vine itself, however, grows quickly and can strangle the life out of other plants, which makes it highly suitable for Hoodoo spells of domination or crossing. Understanding how plants grow is vital to being a good rootworker!

Attracting love is one thing. Sifting through the throngs of people who will come to you after you start using the Love Drawing Oil is another ballgame entirely. This work, using the flowers of the honeysuckle, allows you to find the kind of love that you are in need of.

With this simple rootwork, you can find the proverbial needle in a haystack. It is designed to bring you genuine love. This means that you must mirror the type of love you want. Lose the Hollywood romance plot. Focus on real, unfiltered love and you will attract it to you. Plant the seeds of love in your heart as you whip the tools together. It would put your spirit in the right frame to rec love.

What You Will Need

- Love Drawing Oil
- Red candle
- Honeysuckle flowers

The Work

1. Dress the love candle with the Love Drawing Oil by rubbing the oil on it from top to bottom.
2. Place the candle on a plate on a non-flammable part of your altar.
3. Sprinkle the petals of the honeysuckle flowers around the candle wick and then light it.
4. Center your focus on your intentions (to attract your true love) as you watch the flame burn.

This work draws on your energy and focus. You will focus on the flames, visualize your intentions, vocalize your expectations in the form of the scriptures, and then will them into existence. You must stay at the candle until you can smell the scent of the honeysuckle, and then let the candle burn down naturally. You can speak the Song of Solomon 2:10-13 to aid the work as the candle burns.

LOVE BINDING WITH HOODOO DOLLS

Hoodoo uses dolls as the spiritual stand-in for your target, so whatever you work on the doll manifests physically on that person. You can purchase a doll from a Hoodoo shop, or you can make one yourself. You can even purchase a doll from a toy store, but try to find one that looks like, or reminds you of, your target. For this work, you are simply using the doll to create an opportunity for the two of you to blossom and grow into more than just acquaintances.

The connection between the doll and the person is strengthened by something that represents them, ideally something from their body, such as their hair, their spit, or even their blood. If you can't get any of these, you can use a piece of their clothing or a picture of them. After this item is affixed to the doll, the doll is baptized and brought to life with holy water, which you can purchase online or get for free from a local church.

This working is for when you already know the right person for you, but they don't seem to know you exist. You see them on the street and you exchange a cursory nod, some mumbled greetings, and that's about the extent of your communication. You can change that with this 'Get Noticed' rootwork. It beams the spotlight on you and directs this person's focus to you in the most positive way. You are subtly influencing their emotions or feelings as this rootwork leaves them open to suggestions from you.

What You Will Need

- Two dolls (one for you and one for your target)
- Something to represent your intended
- A lock from your hair
- Something to affix the previous two items to the dolls, such as tape or glue
- Two red candles
- String
- Holy water

The Work

1. Affix your hair to the doll that represents you.
2. Sprinkle the doll's head with the holy water and say, "I baptize you in the name of the Father, and of the Son and of the Holy Spirit." Then give the doll your name. "I name you Angela." Repeat this three times.
3. Repeat this process with the doll representing your target. Use one of the items of theirs that you were able to get (picture/clothing/hair).
4. Light the candles at your altar.
5. Place the dolls on each other and bind them together with string.
6. Speak your intentions (for example, "Notice me, Eric") three times and blow out the candles.

The person whose doll is bound to yours is now bound to you. You can tell them to notice you and they will. As you gain more experience in the craft, you can learn to make the dolls yourself instead of purchasing them.

TURN A FRIENDSHIP INTO LOVE WITH LODESTONES

The most sustainable relationships are those born out of genuine friendships. When you find couples who have been together for decades, one of the secrets to their lasting relationship is their friendship. However, we often find ourselves in situations where we are stuck in the friend zone. When you are in the friend zone, it means that when you talk about the potentials of that relationship, the other person is unable to see beyond friendship. This usually results in one party pining over the other.

This conjure work, to turn friendship into love, requires the use of a lodestone. Lodestones are magnetic rocks. They occur naturally and are particularly useful in attracting what you desire, whether it is a love spell or a money conjure. These mineral stones have gender. So it's important that when you buy a lodestone, it should represent the gender you are interested in converting from friend to lover. Stones with pointy edges are considered masculine, while those with curvier edges are regarded as feminine. Also, every time the stone is able to attract or bring you closer to something that you asked it to do for you, you must feed it with magnetic sands to continue to boost its energy. Whenever I am recommending rootwork for beginners, I like to use conjures that involve lodestone because it is very simple to work with and difficult to get wrong. Despite its simplicity, it is very effective at getting the job done.

This working also uses vervain oil, which is useful in both love and domination spells, as well as in Anointing Oil, making it perfect for this work in which we will use it to anoint the lodestones and compel your intended.

What You Will Need

- Two lodestones (one to represent each person)
- Magnetic sand
- Whiskey
- Vervain oil (to attract love) - a few drops
- Transparent jar

The Work

1. Pour the whiskey into the transparent jar. Ensure that the jar is at least half full or contains enough whiskey to completely submerge the lodestones.
2. Place both lodestones into the whiskey and seal the jar, leaving it overnight.
3. In the morning, take out the lodestones and place them on a flat surface in your altar, letting them dry for a few minutes.
4. As soon as they are dry, take a few drops of the vervain oil and consecrate the lodestones. Do this by rubbing the vervain oil on the lodestone and telling each stone its name, one for you and one for your intended.

5. Tell the lodestones in clear terms what you want them to do for you. For example, "I want Mary to see me as someone she could fall in love with."
6. When you are done, take a pinch of magnetic sand and sprinkle it on the lodestone. Repeat this process at least once every week.

When the stone is completely covered with sand, gently toss the sand off and reinsert the lodestone into the whiskey jar to repeat the process. When the stone is no longer able to attract sand, that means its energy has expired. The best way to discard a lodestone with dead energy is to bury it.

MAKE SOMEONE CALL YOU WITH CIGAR SMOKE

We have all been put in this scenario: you go out to a party or an event and you meet this amazing guy or girl. You exchange numbers and then for days you hear nothing from them. Waiting for this call can be a crushing and devastating blow to your self-esteem, as it projects the perception that this person does not really care about you and probably doesn't want to be with you.

With this rootwork, you don't need to fold your hands and wait. You can stimulate that person's memory of you and get them to pick up the phone and call you. We can also use this work to get that business call we need to come through. It is really that easy.

This spell that I am going to teach you involves the use of cigars. Ancestors love cigar smoke, so we use it to draw their attention to the work and thank them for their help. When we use a cigar in Hoodoo, we light it and get it going, then turn it around and put the lit end into our mouth and blow the smoke out the other side. Please, please be careful with this or you'll end up burning your tongue.

What You Will Need

- Your cell phone
- One white candle
- Cigar
- Chalk
- Salt

The Work

1. Place the cell phone on something you can draw on with the chalk. A wooden table, a driveway or a sidewalk will do.
2. Using the chalk, draw a straight arrow pointing towards the phone.
3. Draw a small circle below the cell phone.
4. Carve the name of the person you want to call you on the candle, then place it in the center of that circle. You can drop a bit of the candle wax into the center of the circle and put the candle on top of the wax to help it stay in place.
5. Use the table salt to draw a line underneath the circle and then light the candle.
6. Light your cigar and get it burning well. Turn the cigar around and put the lit end into your mouth. Avoid your tongue and clench it with your teeth, blowing the smoke out

in a circular motion around the candle and the phone arena you have created.

The arrow will draw the person's energy to your phone, as will the light of the candle. The line of salt below the candle will make sure they can't get around you - their thoughts will have only one place to go.

RESTORE PASSION MOJO BAG WITH DAMIANA

One of the things that keeps a relationship sizzling hot is passion. Remember the days when your partner would walk into a room and you would feel your stomach drop because of all the butterflies in there? Well, as time goes on, these feelings fade and boredom begins to set in. You won't experience the same hot and bothered flushes you had when you first started dating each other.

But this doesn't have to spell doom and gloom for your relationship. You can restore passion. To do that, there are a couple of things you can do, including this rootwork that involves the use of damiana. This is a plant famous for its aphrodisiac qualities (among other things). Some people dry it, grind it into a paste, and put it in their tea. In this work, we'll use the petals in a mojo bag so you can keep it with you.

What You Will Need

- Dried damiana leaves - one tablespoon
- Red rosebuds (to draw love) - one tablespoon
- Lavender buds (for luck in love) - one tablespoon

- Mixing bowl
- Red flannel bag

The Work

1. Put the rosebuds, damiana, and lavender buds in a mixing bowl.
2. Stir the mix thoroughly.
3. As you stir, focus on your intention to bring back passion into your relationship.
4. Pour your mixture into the red flannel bag.
5. Dress the mojo bag with Love Drawing Oil once a week and keep it close to you at all times.

When focusing your intention, you can use these Bible verses to support your cause. For use on a man, read Songs of Solomon 1:2-4. For use on a woman, use Songs of Solomon 7:6-8.

SWEETEN A RELATIONSHIP WITH A SWEET POTATO

There may come a time in your once upon a time 'can't-get-enough-of-each-other' relationship where everything comes to a standstill. You are both stuck with each other but also find that you cannot stand each other.

Relationships often go through different stages and the stage where everything gets boring can last for a very long time. If you are unable to get things back on the sweet track, you risk losing the relationship, and this is something we want to avoid at all costs. The work I am going to share here should only be used for a relationship that you feel has the potential to be something more, and the key ingredient is a sweet potato. Sweet potato is an old Hoodoo staple, and as it grows, so will the sweetness in your relationship. This isn't a spell for someone you're just passing time with, it's for a long and meaningful relationship. If you are sure that the person you are with is worth the work, then let's get some romance cooking.

What You Will Need

- One fresh sweet potato
- A jar
- Brown paper
- A small knife
- Water
- Four toothpicks
- Twine

The Work

1. Write down the names of yourself and your partner on the brown paper.
2. Fold the paper in four and set it aside.
3. Use the knife to make a small incision in the sweet potato somewhere in the middle. Make the incision just big enough to fit the folded-up paper.
4. Insert the folded paper. Ensure that it goes in completely.

5. Wrap the twine around the area of the sweet potato with the insertion and tie it closed.
6. Use the toothpicks to pierce the sweet potato below the twine so that they form an X and can be used to support the sweet potato at the top of the jar, so that half is positioned above the top of the jar and half is inside it.
7. Fill the jar with water.
8. Place the potato in a drawer with the toothpicks serving as a support base to keep the potato upright. Watch for the development of roots at the bottom of the potato and the first signs of growth on top.

As the potato takes root, your relationship will begin to evolve into something sweeter. It may not be exactly as it was in the beginning, but it will be something new and sweet.

REMOVE OUTSIDE INTERFERENCE WITH CANDLE MAGIC

In my experience, when a person exits their current relationship, they are often leaving for another person. This means that many of our relationships come to an end because of external interference. This external interference could manifest in many forms. Sometimes, it is because of an affair or a romantic interest in someone other than you. In other cases, the other person's family may be actively trying to break up your relationship simply because it does not meet their standards or expectations.

The work we are going to do here will be to focus on external interference of the romantic sort. Regardless of your gender, you can put together the items for this work to get rid of this interference so that your true love can keep 100 percent of their attention on you. This will probably be the first advanced candle work you are going to do. Candles are a form of representation magic in Hoodoo work. The color of the candle can set the tone for the spell. Red for passion, pink for romance, and so on. For this kind of work to do its job, you need to have a couple of details on hand before you proceed. Those details include, but are not limited to, the interfering person's name, their date of birth, and (if you can get them) some personal items from your love, such as their hair or nail clippings.

As soon as you have secured the information required for this kind of work, you can proceed. One more thing; the candles that you purchase for this work should be personalized to represent both of you. There are different ways to do that, but the easiest is to buy each candle in the same color as your respective birthstones. If you can't get ahold of those, two white candles will do. Make sure the candles are in glass for this spell, because they will be wrapped in twine or string and we don't want that to catch fire.

What You Will Need

- Two candles in glass to represent you and your love
- A black candle to represent the person interfering
- Twine or string
- Partner's hair or nail clippings (if you can get this)
- Paper bag

The Work

1. Carve your names into the candles that represent you and your love.
2. Carve the name of the person interfering into the black candle.
3. Sprinkle your partner's hair or nail clippings around the top of their own candle.
4. Cut the twine a foot or so in length.
5. Tie each end of the twine around the candles that represent the both of you.
6. Light the two candles. Do not light the black figure candle.
7. As each candle burns, slowly turn both candles inwards. As you do so, the twine will force them to grow closer together until they touch.
8. Meditate on your intentions until you experience contentment.

The light of your candles, and the ever-shortening twine, will draw you and your love to each other, while the unlit black candle will cause your love to stop noticing that other person. After the candles have burned down, place the black figure candle in a paper bag and toss it in a river, to be carried out of your lives forever.

TO BRING A SECRET LOVE INTO THE OPEN

Relationships that are cultivated in secret can be exciting, but as time goes on the excitement wears out and you start to feel like you are trapped in a cage. You are in the relationship of your dreams but you can't tell anyone about it. Being with someone who is afraid to let the whole world know that you are together can quickly turn into a problem. It can be especially difficult when you're ready to tell the world, but your partner is not, and doesn't seem to understand why the situation is so painful.

You don't have to endure that kind of torment alone. With this work, you can make your partner feel the same anguish that you feel, making them ready to bring your love out into the light.

This work uses calamus root, also called sweet flag. A flowering calamus looks like, well, let's just say a man who isn't thinking with his head. Our ancestors noticed things like that and were able to decipher what herbs could be used for which spells, and now calamus is a common herb in Hoodoo love and domination spells.

What You Will Need

- Calamus root powder - three teaspoons
- Salt
- Piece of paper
- A pan

The Work

1. Write both your names on the piece of paper.
2. Put the calamus root on the name paper and fold it closed.
3. Place the folded name paper in a pan and cover it with salt.
4. Place the pan on a stove on medium high heat.

5. When the pan is hot enough that the mixture starts to crackle, call out your lover's name three times.
6. Announce to the spirits that you want your lover to reveal your relationship to the world.

The heat and calamus root, along with the help of your ancestor spirits, will pick at your lover's mind until they do what you want. You can let the mixture cool and then bury it in the ground.

REMIND YOUR PARTNER ABOUT YOUR INITIAL LOVE WITH A PHOTO

Love is a beautiful thing and the first three months of love are the most amazing. You feel as though you are floating on clouds and living in this bubble where nothing can touch you. It is incredible. But as time goes by, over-familiarity seeps in. You hang out together and see the bits and pieces about each other that are not so pleasant.

As a result, the rose-tinted glasses come off, and reality sets in. And when this happens, love does not always stay in the picture. Things get boring. You take each other for granted and the relationship becomes shaky. It is a typical love story in the real world. Everyone goes through it, but if you feel this is the relationship of your dreams and you want to keep things hot and spicy, one way to do that is to return to the way things were in the beginning.

Sometimes, sitting down and reminiscing about the good old days can help reignite those feelings. But what would make this even more effective is if you could put your lover under a spell to make them feel as if you are both back in the early days. A picture freezes a moment in time and captures the emotions. This spell will use that trapped energy to remind your partner of what you once felt for each other.

What You Will Need

- Love Drawing Oil
- Red candle
- Picture of you both together at the start of your relationship

The Work

1. Place the picture on your altar.
2. Soak your mind in the memory that this picture inspires.
3. Dress the red candle in Love Drawing Oil.
4. Carve the initials of your beloved on the candle, light it, and place it next to the picture (be careful not to catch the photo on fire!).
5. Allow the candle to burn out.

This spell picks up on the energy created by a previous memory and the picture that you put on the altar anchors that energy. The spirits of your ancestors will focus on this energy and use it to redirect it back at the person you want to remember how they felt about you in the early days. This is one of those Hoodoo conjures that we have to do at least once a month in order to keep things feeling great.

INCREASE COMMITMENT WITH ORANGE PEELS

Orange peels are very good in control work, especially those spells that beginners do. They have a way of mentally and emotionally clearing blockages. If you have a partner who enjoys being with you but finds it difficult to actually commit to you, conjure work involving orange peels can help push their mind in the direction that you want it to go.

For this spell, we are going to combine orange peels and candles to help illuminate the path for your partner and lead them to the conclusion that they want to spend or invest more time with you. This is the kind of work you do for someone you are serious about. It would be unfair to require a commitment from someone you have no intention of committing to.

While rootwork does not exactly deal with karma and the consequences of one's action, I still like to advocate good will generally when carrying out these conjures. So, before you initiate the rituals that go into this conjure, be absolutely sure you are ready to be committed to this person.

What You Will Need

- Dried orange peels
- White cloth
- Twine
- Tall white candle
- Piece of paper

The Work

1. Set up the white candle at your altar.
2. Write your name and your intended's name on the paper.
3. Place the cloth flat in front of the candle.
4. Put the orange peels and the paper at the center of the cloth and wrap it up with the twine.
5. Let the candle burn for one hour a day.

This work is meant to clear any doubt your partner may have about committing to you. It also puts you in a positive light so that they are more inclined to see all the amazing qualities you have. When they sleep, their mind and thoughts will be imbued with images of you, making them desire to be and connect with you on a deeper level. You can enhance the work by praying Psalm 31.

SPEED UP A RELATIONSHIP WITH GINGER

Relationships go through different stages, and while there is no fixed method of getting from friendship to marriage, it is also necessary to make sure that you are moving forward. You start out as strangers and then become friends. Then you become physically intimate, which makes you lovers and then you usually move to the engagement phase, where you become the fiancé(e). Finally, you become a wife or husband.

The period of time between the stranger phase and when you become a legal spouse varies. I know of couples who went from being strangers to being married within weeks and I have heard of people who took decades to finally marry. You don't have to lean on the other person's sense of timing in order to get to the stage you want. With this spell, you can quickly move through these phases and get to where you want. For this conjure, we are going to use ginger. Ginger has a way of infusing energy into whatever it is added to.

Even when you take it for health purposes, any drink or herbal concoction that has ginger in it has a way of lifting your spirits. In Hoodoo, it energizes the person for whom the rootwork is intended. Remember to put your mind in the right place before you initiate the spell. Going into it with desperation and frustration can alter the course of the spell and possibly render it ineffective. Put your mind in a positive state before you begin.

What You Will Need

- Ginger - one tablespoon
- Dried yarrow flowers (for love) - one tablespoon
- Dried lady's mantle (for faithfulness) - one tablespoon
- Black cohosh extract (for dominance) - five drops
- Licorice root powder (for courage) - one tablespoon
- Red candle
- Jar

The Work

1. Inscribe your partner's name on the candle and light it at the altar.
2. Assemble the herbs and mix them till they become powder.

3. Add the black cohosh extract.
4. Place the powdered herbs in a transparent jar.
5. Speak your intentions clearly and concisely into the flames.
6. Seal the jar when the candle burns out and use it as instructed below.

If you want your partner to propose, sprinkle the herbs in their shoes. This would prompt them to hasten up in their decision to marry you. If you are in a friends-with-benefits situation, the next time you two meet for a tumble, sprinkle the herbs onto the sheets. You can also put a little bit of the herbs in your perfume or laundry detergent to attract serious relationships or hasten commitment if you are single and searching.

BRING SOMEONE TO THE ALTAR WITH CEMENT

We all have that amazing love who checks all the boxes for us when it comes to long-term commitment but the problem is getting them to that point where they actually commit. They might hang out with you and your family often enough to be considered family. They might even know all of your friends and have charmed every single person in your circle. But for some reason, they just don't take the step that shows their commitment to your relationship. This conjure is designed to cement that person in this relationship and get them to be 100 percent in.

It is particularly helpful if you are in a relationship in which you feel you're one of several in their life. In other words, maybe they are looking for other partners while they are actively in a relationship with you. If you want to get them to fully commit by taking that step to the altar, this rootwork is perfect. All you need is some of their hair.

Now, if you are harboring anger or resentment, do not start on the spell, since the energy you are projecting can influence it and misdirect the spirits of your ancestors. Remember the love that brought you to this point where you want to be committed to this person? Focus on it. Enjoy the beautiful aspects of being in love and let that fill you up as you do this work.

What You Will Need

- Foil tray
- Cement
- Red candle
- Partner's hair

The Work

1. In the foil tray, mix the cement according to instructions. It should be almost at the brim.
2. While the cement is still drying, place the red candle in the center of the tray and light it.
3. Roll your partner's hair into a ball and singe it twice with the flame.
4. The third time, allow it to burn. You can drop it into the cement if the flame is getting near your fingers.

5. As the smoke rises and spreads out, speak your intentions into the flame.
6. Leave the candle to burn and melt into the wet cement. When the flames burn out, your work is done.

Inability to make it to the marital altar is a form of commitment phobia. The cement hardens their resolve and the candle wax at the center represents where that resolve is directed; love. To back up your intentions, pray with Ruth 1: 16-17.

FOR CONTROL IN A RELATIONSHIP WITH LICORICE

Sometimes, it is easy to get what you want out of a relationship if you are more in control. You can dictate the terms as well as the direction of the relationship when you have superior power, and that is what the love work here is about. It allows you to exercise total dominance over your partner without demeaning them or causing them any harm.

This love sweetening jar uses licorice to add an element of control. If you've ever taken a whiff from real licorice root, you'll have noticed how strong the smell is, which is why licorice is used for sweetening and compelling.

I've seen a lot of people on the internet use honey in their love sweetening jars, but I usually use sugar water. The problem with honey is that it's slow, so it's good for long-term love work, but if you want something to happen faster, sugar water is the way to go.

What You Will Need

- Dried licorice root - just a pinch
- Damiana root - just a pinch
- Cinnamon stick (to speed the work)
- Small jar
- Piece of paper
- Sugar
- Water
- Small tea candle

The Work

1. Write you and your partner's name on the piece of paper and place it in the jar.
2. Fill the jar about halfway with sugar.
3. Place the licorice and damiana into the jar.
4. Fill the rest of the jar with water.
5. Close the jar and shake it. This will dissolve the sugar.
6. Place the jar on your altar, and place the tea candle on top of the jar.
7. Light the candle and let it burn down.

You can discard the candle after it's burnt out. Shake the jar daily to gain and keep control in your relationship. You can read Hosea 6:1-2 to enhance the work.

END A PARTNER'S BAD HABITS WITH DEVIL'S SHOESTRING

Devil's shoestring is primarily used in protection spells. The goal is to trip the devil so that his mission is never accomplished. For this work, you want to trip your partner up so that they stop their bad habit pronto. When you are in love with someone, it's almost as if they can't do anything wrong. But as you spend more time with them, you start noticing those micro details that you were oblivious to in the initial stages of the relationship. And then there are those glaring bad habits that irritate you.

A proper conjure work can help them overcome these habits and create an environment where love can thrive. When you are constantly irritated and annoyed by someone, it's difficult to enjoy their presence. Also, getting rid of bad habits can help set them on the right path when it comes to their health. But most importantly, it can put your mind at ease. This conjure work is also recommended for people with spouses who find it difficult to keep their pledge to be faithful. It applies to both womanizers and man-ivores.

It is an easy conjure. I used it on someone who struggled with smoking, and also to help a woman rein in her errant man, so he was only committed to their marital bed. There are specific spells that can cripple a person sexually whenever they want to commit sexual acts with anyone other than their significant, but this one is more generic.

What You Will Need

- Two white candles (for the banishing)
- One black candle (for the bad habit)
- Four purple candles (for your willpower)
- Devil's shoestring incense
- Piece of paper
- Picture of your intended

The Work

1. Place a picture of your intended on your altar.
2. Write your petition down on the paper and place it behind the picture.
3. Position the white candles directly in front of your ancestors (or their possession), on a line that spans the width of your altar.
4. Put the black candle at the center of the altar.
5. Place the purple candles around the black candle like a cross.
6. Light the incense and put it between the purple candle at the top of the cross.
7. Leave until the black candles burn out.

When the black candle burns out, bury it in your backyard. This is not a one-time spell and only works to remove the things that might tempt your partner into that specific bad habit. It does not necessarily stop them from doing the thing. It just cuts off their supply, making them more likely to quit in the long term. When the time comes to renew the spell, make sure you use a new set of candles. You can enhance your work with Titus 1:11-12.

PINNING YOUR PARTNER DOWN

Wayward partners are the worst. First, there is the physical betrayal and trauma that comes with that behavior, not to mention the risk of contracting STDs, among other things. Then there is the emotional pain of knowing that someone you love is disregarding the love you have for them. In marital homes, this disregard becomes complete disrespect for the vows that they took at the altar. I take cheating spouses seriously because of my own experiences and also because of what my clients have been through.

But you know what? If you love that idiot so much and you think that your relationship is worth saving, you can use conjure work to keep their sexual organs only functional when it comes to you. For this rootwork, we are going to use dolls and pins. This is one of the most common forms of keeping a straying partner at home. I like it because it is simple, effective, and can be turned on and off. So, if you have a partner who you are sure is cheating, you can make a doll and fix it in a way that whenever your partner goes to have sexual relations with someone other than you, they will not be able to perform as expected.

What You Will Need

- Hoodoo doll
- Tailor pin (for a man)
- Candle (for a woman)

- Holy water
- Pubic hair of the target

The Work

1. Place the pubic hair of the target on the doll for potency. The pubic hair should be placed on the corresponding genital area of the doll.
2. Bind the doll to the target by sprinkling the doll's head thrice with holy water and repeating these words, "I name you (insert target's name). You are now this doll and this doll is you."
3. For a man, pierce the genital area of the doll with the pin, but make sure it doesn't go through the doll. Then tell the doll what you want.
4. For the woman, place the genitals of the dolls over a burning candle. Call her name three times and speak your intentions to the flames. Don't let it burn. The result might be permanent.
5. Keep the doll in a safe space.

Whenever you want to have intercourse with your partner, take out the pin for the man. For the woman, place a ball of wet cotton wool on the doll's genitals. Relations should proceed as usual. When they go out and you suspect their intentions, simply run through steps 3 or 4 and then repeat step five.

BRING A LOVER BACK WITH TWINE

The spell we are going to use in this rootwork is designed to work on partners who are indecisive and have a habit of breaking things off and then returning to you, only to repeat that again and again. To save yourself the heartache, it's better to simply pull them in and ensure that they stay in. This conjure is different from getting a person to commit, as it is more about returning them to your arms.

Twine is used like bindings in many Hoodoo workings. It symbolizes the bond between things, or can be used to prevent an enemy from making any moves. If you only have plain string in your home, that's completely fine - use what you have.

I remember doing this for a client who had been in and out of a relationship for more than half a decade. It got to a point where she was done with the constant heartbreaks and wanted to seal the relationship once and for all. This was a particularly poignant situation for her because he had abandoned her and their one-year-old daughter. She decided she wasn't ready to have her daughter go through the same thing she had been going through. I understood her concerns, so we set to work.

Through this work with candle and twine, you can reel your lover back in and, in the process, hopefully remind him of what he's missing at home.

What You Will Need:

- Two white candles (to represent you and your target)
- Twine

The Work:

1. Assign the candles to both of you by inscribing your names on them. One for you and the other for your significant other.
2. Cut about a foot of twine and tie each end to a candle.
3. Light the candles and speak your intentions into the flames.
4. Turn the candles inwards toward each other until they meet.
5. Put out the candles when you experience closure. Store the candles in your closet.

This conjure is similar to the one for blocking out interference, except that you are not using black figure candles and the candles that you lit can remain at the altar. To empower your spells, I suggest doing a cleansing bath before you start this work.

END CONFLICT WITH SUGAR

Sugar has a restorative quality and can sweeten almost anything. Lemons, coffee, a sour relationship… it is excellent for conjure works focused on removing bitterness and conflicts. Conflicts are inevitable. Even in a relationship that is considered perfect by all accounts, the parties are bound to have a disagreement at some point. The hallmark of a healthy relationship is not the absence of conflict but the ability to resolve things amicably without degradation or abuse. Sadly, there are times in a relationship when both partners behave like cats and dogs - arguing constantly, divided at every turn, and seemingly unable to reach a satisfactory compromise on anything.

When conflict goes on for too long, it leads to a breakup. If you find that dialogue, as well as other means of communication (including mediation by external influences), has not brought you and your partner any closer together, and you are certain that this relationship is what you want, a spell to end conflict might be what you need.

This spell tears down walls erected by pride, suspicions, poor communication, and so on, giving both parties an opportunity to bury the hatchet and make an attempt to know and understand each other better. Burying your work is a very symbolic act. You use it to put an end to something, close a chapter or keep something out of sight.

What You Will Need

- Sugar - one teaspoon
- Vanilla extract (to calm troubles) - one teaspoon
- Lavender essential oil (for luck in love) - a few drops
- A small blue candle
- A jar filled with water

The Work

1. Poke three holes through the top of the blue candle.
2. Pour a few drops of lavender oil, vanilla extract, and sugar into each hole.
3. Place the candle at the center of your altar and light it.
4. Speak your intentions as the candle burns.
5. When the candle burns out, put the candle ends inside the jar of water.
6. Seal the jar tightly and bury it in your backyard.

Blue candles are used for bringing healing to relationships. When your relationship is gripped with strife, putting an end to the conflict is one way to put things back on track and restore peace. When the sealed jar goes into the ground, so does the conflict. When you cover it with dirt, the conflict is as good as gone. Do not break this jar. You can enhance the work with Psalm 32.

SMOOTH OUT RECONCILIATION WITH WORMWOOD

Wormwood is a powerful spiritual herb. It is used in powerful protection spells and to promote mental and spiritual healing. Sometimes, you need a little help to get you to a place where you can smooth things over with your partner.

Let's say you've gotten into a serious conflict but have done your best to bring it to an end. You don't just want it to be closed and never spoken about again, but you want to make sure you both have closure and the healing you need to move forward. This conjure work can make that happen. You need a pink love candle and wormwood. The most important ingredient for this spell, though, is your state of mind. You have to let go of any residual anger or resentment. You must put yourself in a forgiving mood.

To make things even better, put your mind in a love trance. Listen to some good love songs. Remember the days when the love was super sweet between you and your significant other. Don't make this conjure work about the situation or source of conflict. Your focus should be on smoothing out your relationship. Ask yourself, if it works out the way you want, how do you plan to enjoy your relationship going forward? The answers might give you some extra incentive and a spirit boost to your spell power.

What You Will Need

- Wormwood powder or dried leaves - a few teaspoons
- Honey (to sweeten)
- Pink candle
- Eight pins

The Work

1. Carve the name of your beloved on the candle.
2. Dip all eight pins in honey.
3. Stick each pin into the base of the candle to form a halo.
4. Scatter wormwood at the top of the candle and then light it.
5. As the smoke rises, pray for swift reconciliation. If your

beloved is mad at you, they will be visited with dreams about you that will turn away their anger and change their mind.

Give this spell an hour before putting out the candle. Repeat it every day for nine days. If a candle finishes, bless a new candle and repeat the process. On the ninth day, thank your ancestors for a successful job. Pack all the burned candles, wash them under running water and dispose of them.

MAKE THINGS FUN AGAIN WITH RINGS

The spell we're going to work here is two-fold. The first is for people who are in relationships and would like to strengthen them and move towards marriage. The conjure works by igniting the spark that was there in the beginning. The second use is for couples who are already married and would like to heal whatever rifts have taken place during their marriage. Both works require the use of rings.

It doesn't matter if you are not engaged and therefore have no ring in the first category. You can use an old ring to carry out the spell. For the married couple, you will use your wedding ring to activate the spell. Two ingredients, basil and mint, will be used for this spell. You can use both of them together or separately. I like them together because while mint refreshes and invigorates, basil works with what you already have. This means that mint can be used when you are trying to bring something new into your life, while basil grounds the work in the love you already have.

In essence, if you have a relationship that is already ongoing, basil will make sure that those new sensations and feelings you want have been activated in that relationship. It is pretty straightforward and very simple. Just grab a ring and we're ready to go.

For unmarried couples

What You Will Need

- Old ring
- Mint leaves (to refreshen)
- Basil leaves (to enhance)

The Work:

1. Place the ring on the altar.
2. Wrap the ring in fresh basil and mint leaves.
3. Leave the ring on the altar overnight.
4. Put the ring under your lover's pillow on the bed that you share.

For married couples

What You Will Need:

- Your wedding ring
- Jar
- Sugar (to sweeten)
- Mint
- Basil

The Work:

1. Pour sugar generously into the jar.
2. Put your ring inside the jar.
3. In a small bowl, crush the mint, sugar, and basil together. You want the flavor of the mint and basil to be absorbed into the sugar.
4. Pour the mixture on top of the ring in the sugar jar.
5. Leave it overnight in the kitchen of the home you share.

In the morning, you can take the ring out and toss the remnants of the spell. Repeat this routine once a month to maintain a constant flow of the fun and invigorating power that this work brings to your home and marriage. However, if the arguments are getting too frequent and you keep creating spells to end the conflict, you might want to think about the source of the issue and see if you can fix it.

PUT AN END TO STUBBORNNESS WITH ORCHIDS

This conjure work is particularly suited for females. So, if you are a woman with a partner who is extremely stubborn, this is the conjure work that you can use to end their stubbornness. It establishes your dominance over them in a relationship and puts the control in your hands. Through this spell, you will be able to get your partner to become docile and submissive towards you. And when you are more in control of the relationship, you can put an end to a lot of the things that cause problems, because your partner will be more willing to follow your wishes and live by your principles.

The most important ingredient for the spell is a live orchid. Orchids are a beautiful flower associated with femininity. If you can find a wild orchid, great, but if not, you can plant one somewhere and it will work just as well.

What You Will Need

- Live orchid
- Piece of paper

The Work

1. Write down the name of your intended target and their birthday three times.
2. Fold the paper towards you.
3. Clearly voice your intentions and bury the name paper at the foot of the live orchid.

The growing orchid will cause your man to be more compliant with your wishes. Where he was previously ferocious and stubborn, he will become gentle and docile. Where he was adamant and unforgiving, he will become receptive and agreeable. This does not turn him into a doormat. Far from it. It merely puts an end to those unnecessary arguments.

END OVER-POSSESSIVENESS WITH BURLAP

When a burlap sack is thrown over a person's head, their vision is immediately restricted. They become oblivious to what is happening around them. As a result, their perception of control becomes altered. This is exactly what you want to do to an over-jealous lover. When I was younger, I have to admit I found a little bit of possessiveness attractive. I liked the idea of my man going crazy at the very thought of another man attempting to flirt with me, even though I had no intention of following through. Jealousy can give off those romantic cowboy story vibes.

That said, when you are in a relationship someone who takes things too far when it comes to possessiveness, it becomes a huge issue and is time to check that trait. Normally, I would encourage you to walk out of any relationship that causes you to suffer any form of abuse. But if you feel that, apart from being overly possessive, your partner has other redeeming qualities, a spell like this can shut down that jealous nature, allowing those other wonderful qualities to shine through.

What You Will Need

- Hoodoo doll
- Burlap cloth (small piece)
- Twine
- Target's hair
- Holy water

The Work

1. Sprinkle the doll's head three times with holy water, and say "I name you (your target's name)."
2. Attach some of your partner's hair to the doll.

3. Place the burlap cloth over the doll's head.
4. Tie the cloth at the back of the doll's head with a small piece of twine.
5. Speak your intentions. For instance, you can tell the doll to stop being paranoid, or to not focus on you so much.
6. Place the doll in a dark place.

With this work, your partner becomes blind to your actions and therefore has no reason to suspect you of anything, much less be jealous. They are oblivious to your flaws and will never hold your shortcomings against you. Understand this, the spell does not rid them of their possessive nature. As I said earlier, it simply shuts them down by turning off their triggers. If their nature causes them to be volatile, get them to seek help, or better still, quit the relationship while you can. You can enhance the work with Psalm 39.

END A RELATIONSHIP WITH A POTATO

Did you know that new potatoes can grow out of old ones? It is symbolic that something new can be born out of the end of something else. Breakups can be painful but this spell ends an existing relationship in a way that lets each person move on to a new phase of their life. And it doesn't have to be the breakup of your own relationship. Perhaps the person you are with is still holding on to an old relationship. We can use the spell to break things off so that he or she can focus fully on you.

It is inevitable that if you have done everything you can to help your relationship thrive and have still failed, you reach a point where the only way forward is to go your separate ways. You must embrace this reality and let go. But breaking up is easier said than done. Telling another person that you are about to sever the connection you have with them can be devastating.

It's important to acknowledge that even though you are the one initiating the break-up, that doesn't mean you are not hurting. Another benefit of the spell we are going to create is that it will try to smooth things over and make the break-up process easier. This is why we are using a white potato as the base for the spell; unlike the sweet potato rootwork that is supposed to sweeten a relationship, here we are breaking things up as delicately as possible.

What You Will Need

- A piece of paper
- Green onion
- White potato
- Twine

The Work

1. Write the names of the couple on the paper. One name should be written horizontally and the other vertically to form a cross.
2. Fold the paper. Lay it forward once. Turn it counterclockwise and fold it away from you once again. Repeat this two more times. Set it aside.
3. Cut the potato from the bottom to the top but not all the

way through. The gap should be wide enough to house the green onions. Set it down.
4. Hold the green onion in your hands and focus on your intention.
5. Call the name of your partner and the name of the person you are breaking them apart from, whether it's you or someone else.
6. Split the green onion into two vertical halves.
7. Insert the name paper in between the split onions.
8. Insert the onion and paper in the potato.
9. Tie the potato and onions with twine to secure everything in place.
10. Bury it somewhere the potatoes and onions can grow.

Breaking up a couple other than yourself is a bit of a controversial topic. But I prefer to look at it on a case-by-case basis. Every relationship has its own 'DNA', so the story differs from person to person. The only ones qualified to judge the situation are those involved. So, when you dabble in conjure work that breaks other people apart, try as much as possible not to latch on to the negative judgment of other people. It can create an energy that works against your intentions. Be confident in your decisions.

GET RID OF UNWANTED ATTENTION WITH LEMONS

Lemons are used for spells to turn things sour. If a person is giving you too much unwanted attention, a little lemon can turn things sour and cause them to back off. Nobody wants to be at the receiving end of attention that they do not want.

I had a client who struggled through years of harassment from someone who was totally obsessed with her. She moved to four cities and changed jobs even more than that to escape his attentions. But somehow, he would always find her. She was so psychologically and emotionally damaged by the experience that she could barely function in society. By the time she came to me, she was a complete emotional wreck. Even though she had changed her number more than ten times, this stalker would find her number and resume calling her.

She had reached the end of her rope when she came to me, so I did this conjure for her. This was a man who had harassed her every single day for more than two years. But within nine days of the conjure, the man had vanished from her life, and for the first time she was truly free. If you want someone to stop thinking about you and showering you with unwanted attention, perform the spell and your problem will be solved.

What You Will Need

- Four burned matches
- Empty jar
- A piece of paper
- Lemon cut in half
- Onion peel
- Black feather
- String

The Work

1. Write the name and birthday of the target on the paper.
2. Fold the paper.
3. Wrap the name paper around the black feathers and tie it with string.
4. Place the lemon face up inside the jar.
5. Put the onion peel on top of the lemon.
6. Arrange the matches on top of the onion peel like kindling.
7. Poke the feather into the middle of the pile and leave it standing upright.
8. Fill the jar with water and close the lid tight. You may have to push the feather down to get the jar to close.
9. Shake the jar vigorously and call the name of the person whose attention you want to end. Say this, "Leave my life. Take your strife. In this life and in the next, may our paths never cross." Do this nine times.
10. Take the jar far away from your home. The farther away, the better. Bury it in the ground and the job is done.

When you want to cut off the attention of someone, you have to do it mentally just as you have done it physically. In other words, you also have to cut them off in your mind. Reminiscing about the attention they gave you can weaken the energy you put into the creation of the spell. You see, your ancestors latch onto your emotions and intentions when helping you to fulfill the purpose of the spell. When they sense that you are thinking about this person, it weakens your hold on your spirit guide and might also weaken the spell. Bury the jar in the ground and bury this person in your thoughts at the same time.

STOP LOVING SOMEONE AT THE CROSSROADS

It is important to understand that there are spirits at crossroads. If you are going to be practicing crossroad spells, you must familiarize yourself with the spirit by frequently bringing offerings to it. Don't wait until you need to do a conjure before you give that offering. This would make the spirit more inclined to help. Also, when you speak the words in step 3 below, be mindful of two things: Do you want the spell to be permanent or temporary? For a permanent outcome, give an impossible condition, like "until the sun rises in the west." For a temporary outcome, the condition could be something that is fulfilled by the other person, such as, "until he/she loves me unconditionally."

The heart wants what it wants. People say that love is just a chemical reaction in your brain or that it is the stirring in your loins that inspires love. But when you look at it objectively, people in love can seem very stupid at times. A person who is normally perfectly logical will start making seemingly irrational decisions in the name of love. In itself, this can be quite harmless, unless the object of their affection turns out to be ruthless and takes everything they have to offer. In this case, love becomes poison.

You have probably heard stories of people who were completely ruined by love. The problem is not that they fell in love. The problem is the person with whom they fell in love. They probably know that this person is no good for them, but try as they might, as I said, the heart wants what it wants. There is no reasoning or logic to this type of love. If you are in that situation and you want to stop being in love with someone, this is what you should do.

What You Will Need

- Charcoal powder (for banishing) - one tablespoon
- Red rose petals (to tie the banishment to love) - a handful
- Salt (for purification) – half a tablespoon
- Three pennies

The Work

1. Put the rose petals, charcoal, and salt in a mortar and grind the materials until they become a paste. You can add a bit of water to help.
2. Say these words, "My love for (insert object of love's name), I banish you. Never to return until… (insert a condition)."
3. Take the mixture with you to a crossroads.
4. Bury the pennies in the dirt near the crossroads, and thank the spirit for its help.
5. Using the mixture, at the center of the crossroads draw a circle and four arrows pointing away from the circle.
6. Spit in the center of the circle. Turn around and walk away.

Before we move on, I want to point out something. By admitting that the love you have for this person is destroying you, you have made progress. Don't block out the pain. Give yourself time to heal and then move on.

5

SPELLS FOR MONEY AND SUCCESS

Money is a necessity that we cannot do without. It is virtually impossible to get from point A to point B without some form of financial assistance or transaction along the way. The world we operate in today speaks a universal language and that language is money.

Some people have wrongfully ascribed the word 'evil' to money. I am sure you've probably heard the phrase, "money is the root of all evil." It is this kind of thinking that has caused a lot of people to develop an unhealthy relationship with money. This unhealthy relationship feeds their attitude towards money, and when you don't have the right attitude towards money, it is difficult to attract it into your life.

Money is manifested through energy. The most common form of energy expended to manifest money is physical energy through labor. This is the one we are taught from birth to use. But what many don't know is that you can also focus your mental energy to attract money to you through conjure work.

With the combination of that dark Hollywood narrative on Hoodoo and the many cautionary tales passed on to us by parents and guardians, we see money obtained through conjures and rootwork as tainted. It is almost as if we find it hard to accept money unless we labor for it. But here is the thing with rootwork: it is not limited to specific functions. In fact, I believe we have not even tapped a quarter of the financial resources that the powers of our ancestors have made available to us. If you can sit in your house and create a conjure work that attracts a man to your doorstep, how then is it difficult for you to accept that you can invoke the spirit of money and demand it to work for you?

I always have ongoing money work on my altar. I like to use the green candle with honeysuckle leaves (I'll talk about that spell later on). This conjure work ensures that I have an abundance of money. You see, I don't just want to get by. I want to thrive and enjoy my life. I know that money can play a role in this dream that I have and I'm not ashamed of it. Neither should you be ashamed of your financial ambition. People associate poverty with piety, not realizing that wealth is a birthright and when you channel your ancestors to access what is rightfully yours, you will unlock the keys to a life without lack.

Before you begin any rootwork in this chapter, I want you to do a little reprogramming exercise to rid yourself of any negative perspectives you have about money. Accept that money is neither your friend nor your enemy. You must also train yourself to have discipline when it comes to money. If you don't have discipline, you will burn through money faster than you can make it and not even your ancestors can help you there.

END BAD LUCK WITH AN ORANGE

Oranges are associated with success in Hoodoo work. If you have been having a bit of a bad run lately, this conjure work is the first place to start. It will reverse any bad luck you have had and usher in positive energy that will activate good luck going forward. I recommend it as an excellent starting point for all your money spells.

First, it invites success into your space. Then it ensures that the success you achieve is accompanied by joy. In my opinion, orange has an incredibly positive vibe and I always love working with it. If oranges are not your thing, you can try to substitute them with some other sweet citrus fruit, like tangerines. Do not use grapefruit or bitter lemon. Those can turn things sour and that is the last thing we want for this spell.

What You Will Need

- One whole orange
- Piece of paper
- Knife
- Salt

The Work

1. Write your full name vertically three times on the paper. Beside each name, write your birthday.
2. Fold the name paper towards you
3. Make an incision in the orange.
4. Insert your name paper into the incision and put the salt on top of it to close off the cut.
5. Hang the orange over the main door of your home. If you live in a shared apartment, hang it over your room door. Leave it there for eight days.
6. On the ninth day, bury the orange. Your work is done.

You can enhance the work with Psalm 90 and verse 91 while the orange hangs over your door.

MONEY DRAWING OIL WITH PEPPERMINT

After a bad luck reversal spell, the next step is to create Money Drawing Oil that will attract money to you but can also be used in the development of some of the other spells that will ensure money freely comes into your home. There are many recipes for Money Drawing Oil, but for this conjure work, I decided to develop something very simple, straightforward and effective. The key ingredient for this work is peppermint.

In Hoodoo, peppermint is a harbinger of good fortune, and it opens up the path for wealth and prosperity to flow into your life. When combined with dried thyme leaves and pyrite powder, it creates a potent money attraction spell, and that's exactly what we are going to do.

What You Will Need:

- Peppermint leaves (for good fortune) - two tablespoons
- Dried thyme leaves (to increase money) - one tablespoon
- Pyrite powder (for abundance) - one teaspoon
- Ground cinnamon (to speed the work) - one teaspoon
- Base oil (Sunflower, almond, even regular cooking oil)
- Green jar

The Work:

1. Bruise the peppermint leaves gently to activate the scent.
2. Pour the peppermint, thyme, and pyrite powder into the jar.
3. Top up the mixture with your base oil.
4. Shake the container to mix the ingredients and then allow the bottle to sit at your altar overnight.

Use generously in your other conjures to speed up answers to your money requests.

ROAD OPENING RITUAL

Sometimes you'll know where you want to get, but find yourself blocked from getting there. Maybe you're blocked by circumstances, or blocked by a person, or maybe you've even put roadblocks in your own way. In Hoodoo, we perform a Road Opening to clear the way.

You can do a Road Opening at any time, but in the South, we do one at the start of every new year. As you'll see, many Southerners are doing Hoodoo Road Openings on New Year's without even realizing it's Hoodoo. Sometimes there isn't much difference between what's "Hoodoo" and what's just "Southern"!

One important item on your to-do list is to prepare and eat a meal that involves cornbread, black-eyed peas, and collard greens. The golden cornbread symbolizes great wealth. Collard greens, with their color and texture, symbolize prosperity. And the black-eyed peas represent abundance.

You'll also take a spiritual bath with sunflower and yellow rose petals, to cleanse your spirit and get ready for a fresh start. Sunflowers absorb all that sunlight and represent joy, happiness, social and material wealth and integrity. Yellow roses represent new beginnings and abundance. Each of the things that they represent are key elements that you want to manifest in the financial aspect of your life when you are opening a path for yourself.

You'll also be burning something from your past. It can be almost anything you're willing to part with - a pay stub from a bad job, a bill you can't pay, a photo of an ex-lover, or even just some old clothes that are holding onto the energy of the past.

What You Will Need:

- Something from your past to burn
- Two white candles
- Offering (food that your ancestors are known to be fond of)

- Sunflower petals - from eight flowers
- Sunflower seeds - one cup (including the seeds from the eight flowers)
- Yellow rose petals - one cup

The Work

1. Start the day by burning white candles at your altar.
2. Present your ancestors with an offering of their favorite food. If you're unsure what to use, go with cake.
3. Thank them for their guidance in the past and express gratitude for their presence in the new year.
4. Sit with them at the altar till the candles burn out.
5. Prepare the meal for the day that includes cornbread, black-eye peas, and collard greens.
6. When you eat, include an extra place setting for your ancestors.
7. In a pot, add the sunflower petals, rose petals and sunflower seeds.
8. Pour water in the pot and leave to boil for about 15 minutes.
9. Strain the petals and seeds from the water.
10. Bathe with the water and use the petals as a sponge. Air dry when you are done.
11. Take the item from your past, along with the used petals, and toss it all into a fire. It can be in your fireplace or a charcoal pit.
12. Allow everything to burn into ashes and let it cool.
13. When it has cooled, gather up the ashes and blow them into

the four different directions of the earth; north, south, east, and west.
14. Take the sunflower seeds and speak all your troubles into them.
15. Put the seeds in a bird feeder or throw them where birds are sure to eat them. When they do, all your troubles will be eaten away. Do all of this before midnight.

You can do this at the start of a new month, or the start of a new week. But it is most powerful when you do it at the start of a new year. Please note, the offerings to your ancestors and the additional plate setting can be thrown away the next day.

THE GREEN MONEY MOJO BAG WITH PINE NEEDLES

It was my grandmother, Mama Estelle, who taught me that money is a type of energy. All that work that people do to get it, all that time spent accumulating it, all that emotion that goes into holding onto it - it's all energy that you can draw to yourself. But Mama Estelle also taught me that money also has a spirit - a hungry spirit - and if you spend too much energy trying to get money, it will consume you. You need to draw it to you and control it, not let it control your life.

There are many roots that work with money - drawing it, protecting it, and growing it, but one of my favorites is pine needles. The pine tree is "evergreen", just like you want your money to be. It can grow in harsh conditions, and it survives even in the cold of winter. All that makes it perfect to use in a money mojo bag that you can keep with you.

What You Will Need

- Pine needles
- Iron pyrite (to draw wealth)
- A piece of paper and a pen
- Three pennies
- Green cloth bag
- String or twine

The Work

1. Write down your name and birthdate on the paper three times on three different lines.
2. Use a hard object to crush the pine needles to let out their scent.
3. Rub the crushed needles on the coins and iron pyrite.
4. Tuck the coins, needles, and iron pyrite into the name paper and fold to completely conceal everything.
5. Put the folded paper into the green cloth bag and tie it all closed.
6. Leave it on your altar overnight.

You can carry this mojo bag around with you, so it can be working on you all the time. Feed the mojo bag three drops of rum once per week to keep the spirit active. Or, if you're taking it gambling, feed it ahead of going out.

QUICK MONEY WITH NUTMEG

Emergencies, whether they are health-related, or due to a failure in business dealings, or even death, are things that you cannot properly plan for. You may be able to save up some money in your emergency account but that will only get you so far. This spell is designed to help you call forth quick cash when you are caught in such situations.

The star ingredient for this spell is nutmeg. Nutmeg is known as a spice that hastens the spirit's response to money requests. With this spell, you can ask your ancestors for help and they will respond swiftly. The amount of money that you can petition for has a limit, though.

You cannot ask beyond what you need at that moment. That is why it's called a quick money spell. It won't make you so rich that you don't need to work ever again. It simply takes care of whatever problems you need to solve immediately.

What You Will Need

- Nutmeg powder - one tablespoon
- Fresh bay leaves (to bring success) - five leaves
- Cinnamon powder (to speed the work) - one tablespoon
- Green candle
- Bowl
- A fire

The Work

1. Gather all the ingredients together in a small bowl.
2. Inscribe your name on the green candle and light it.
3. Speak over the ingredients with your intention. Be clear, concise, and straight to the point when making your petition known.
4. Toss all the ingredients into a burning flame.
5. Hold the candle in front of you and stand in the direction where the smoke from the flames is going. Let it wash over you.
6. When the fire burns out, the spell is done. Put away the candle and be expectant.

The key to this work is to be specific. It helps to focus on the exact amount of cash you need.

ANCESTOR MONEY TREE

When you need some money help from your ancestors, you can leave money on your ancestor altar. That alone helps direct the spirits to provide you financial aid, but you can take it a step further, too. Money doesn't normally grow on trees, but in Hoodoo, it can.

Money that has been left on your altar (I recommend at least three days) can be used to make a Hoodoo Money Tree. Take that ancestor money and combine it with the vitality of a living plant to bring prosperity. When you are in need of cash or are looking to improve your financial health, this money comes in very handy. Of course, your ancestors do not take the physical cash away. Instead, there is an exchange.

Your offerings and prayers are accepted and their essence is poured into the money. When this happens, the money takes on the ability to grow literally and it becomes a conduit through which they (your ancestors) can offer you more.

What You Will Need

- Ancestor money
- A leafy indoor plant
- Transparent tape

The Work

1. Position the indoor plant where it can receive the maximum amount of sunlight that it needs to thrive.
2. Take a few bills from the money at the altar. Cut a small piece of tape, stick one end on the money and the other end on the leaf of a plant. It should look like money is growing off the plant.
3. Say something along the lines of these words, "I am experiencing abundance this season. Whatever I spend, double returns."
4. When you need cash urgently, take a single bill from this tree and spend it.

Feed, water, and care for the plant the same way you would a normal house plant, but, in addition, you should feed it some holy water at least once a month. Do not over-trim the plant, and whenever you take money from the tree, endeavor to replace it when you get a bill that matches the one you took. This new money should first sit on the altar, though.

FAVOR COLOGNE WITH RUM

I love a good conjure that works with rum. Whenever I use it in my works, the energy I get from my ancestors is excitement. There is a certain fervor and willingness that I sense during these works. It's as if they are more than happy to answer my petition. And, I admit, I take a little nip of rum for myself!

In Africa, rum and dry gin are frequently used to get elders to do favors. I am guessing that being in the afterlife increases their fondness for it. This cologne we will create here is perfect for days when you have an interview or you are giving a presentation for a finance-related project.

If you are in the contract business, you can spray a little of this over any written material that will be used in your communique. Also, dabbing this cologne on you before you leave your house can attract financial favors to you.

What You Will Need

- One long strand of orange peel from an orange
- A small bottle of rum

- Your own perfume or cologne
- Nine whole nutmegs

The Work

1. Put the orange peel inside the bottle of rum.
2. Place the nutmegs inside the rum one at a time, each time speaking to it before dropping it. You can say, "Bring me financial favor from far and wide. Let wealth and abundance dwell by my side."
3. Seal the bottle and shake vigorously.
4. Set the bottle in the sun for nine days.
5. At the end of the ninth day, mix some of the work with your perfume. Use whenever you need it.

Another way to use this work is to rub it on money candles for petition. Just make sure that you don't light the candle until it is dry. Rum is flammable!

DISSOLVE DEBTS WITH ONIONS

In Hoodoo, onions are excellent for dissolving, unblocking or dispelling curses. In situations where your life has been under a powerful generational curse, you will use onions in combination with other herbs to break those free. But for a simple money or relationship fix, an onion on its own will do the job.

If you are in a relationship with a person who is trying to put up walls and prevent you from getting into their heart, an onion spell will break down those walls and give you passage. If you are suffering from a mountain of debt, using onions in your conjure can reduce that mountain to rubble. On your journey to financial freedom, you want to break out of the prison of debt.

Whether it is school loans, loans that we have taken from other people, upcoming bills, credit card debt or anything else, this conjure can make it dissolve and offer you the freedom to start fresh and create a new template for a life of wealth and abundance.

What You Will Need

- Two red onions
- Piece of paper
- Pen
- Knife
- A fire

The Work

1. Write down the name of the person or business to whom you owe money nine times.
2. Turn the paper a quarter of the way counter-clockwise.
3. Write the amount that you owe backwards nine times.
4. Fold the paper in two away from you.
5. Put the folded paper on fire and burn it to ash.
6. Gather and set aside the ashes. It's okay if they contains ashes of the wood used to make the fire.

7. Use the knife and cut the two red onions into two equal halves from top to bottom.
8. Smear the insides of the four halves of the cut onions with the ashes from the name paper.
9. Position each half onion in one of the four corners of your house with the insides facing the wall.

As the onions disintegrate and rot, so will the debts linked to the conjure. You will have to do a separate conjure for every debt.

PAY ME BACK WITH HOT PEPPER

For the most part, pepper is used in Hoodoo work to create discomfort in the life of your target. This is very useful if your intention is to cause a breakup, or to irritate or frustrate someone for reasons best known to you.

In this case, if there is someone to whom you loaned money or perhaps carried out a business transaction but they have refused to pay you, throwing some hot pepper into the conjure work will make their life difficult until they fulfill the condition, which is to pay you back. One thing you should know about using hot pepper in conjure work is that it doesn't last very long (thankfully).

The suffering that the person is going to endure will not be indefinite. There is a timeline to it, which is perfect. The idea is not to make them suffer; just motivate them to pay you faster. If your intentions are concise and clear, they will understand that their current predicament is as a result of their failure to fulfill their debt to you. Quick tip; the hotter the pepper, the more fiery the spell will be.

This work also uses a wooden box, which is often used to trap the spirit of someone in an uncomfortable situation. If you don't have a wooden box, a cardboard box or even a shoebox will do.

What You Will Need

- A picture of the target
- Two extra spicy peppers
- Turmeric - one teaspoon
- Ginger - one bulb
- A small wooden box

The Work

1. Place the picture of the person in the wooden box.
2. Mash the peppers into a paste. You may want to use plastic gloves, and be careful not to touch your eyes until you've washed your hands.
3. Put the turmeric, ginger, and pepper on top of the picture.
4. Cover the wooden box and say something along these lines, "<name of your target>, feel the heat and pain until you pay me back."
5. Place the wooden box in a prominent location where sunlight can hit it during the day. Leave it there until the person responds to your demand.

As long as the person has not paid the money, whenever you see the box, imagine them suffering or experiencing physical discomfort. Your ancestral spirits will convey your thoughts and put them into action. But as soon as the person pays, make sure that you empty the box. Throw away the tools for the work, tear the picture or burn it, and thank the ancestors for their work.

PROSPER ME WASH WITH LEMONGRASS

This simple version of a floor wash is something you can do to bring prosperity to a home or business. I recommend doing it once a week for five weeks. What this does is attracts people to your business, bring excellent opportunities your way, and create an environment in which you can thrive financially.

To set up the tools for this conjure, we are going to use lemongrass. In Hoodoo work, lemongrass is used to open the road and attract opportunities. To supplement its work, we are going to use the magnolia flower and peppermint, which help sweeten and radiate positive energy, respectively.

What You Will Need

- Magnolia flowers (handful)
- Lemongrass (handful)
- Peppermint (handful)
- Water (three quarts)
- Pot

The Work

1. Put all the herbs and the water inside the pot and bring to a boil.
2. Stir the contents of the pot until it is boiling.
3. Think of the results that you want as you stir and communicate that to your ancestors.
4. After about half the water has boiled away, strain the herbs from the water.
5. Bury the herbs or wash them away under running water.
6. Use the water to wash the floors of your home or business. Be sure to wash the doors, walls, windows and frames, as well.

As always, your mindset plays an important role in this conjure work. Try to maintain a positive attitude as you do the wash.

GET INSPIRATION WITH CLARITY OIL

Sometimes what you need most is clarity about a situation, but in business it can be hard to separate yourself from the situation. This work will bring you the inspiration you need, and uses Clarity Oil to clear the way, and candles to bring new ideas.

A spell like this will train your intuition to act like a hound hunting down a specific scent. It will follow the trail that will lead you to what you seek. It is also useful for setting specific goals and creating the right mental atmosphere that will allow you to achieve those goals. This Hoodoo work requires absolute focus.

For this work, you will have to do things one goal at a time. When you have successfully achieved your first goal, you can move on to the next on your list. Don't worry, the process for setting the spell is quick, so you should be able to achieve your goals within a reasonable timeline.

First, you must make your Clarity Oil. This recipe is a small batch, good for just this one working, but you can scale up the ingredients if you'd like. For this you need essential oils of the following herbs:

- Pine (three drops)
- Rosemary (three drops)
- Sage (three drops)
- Carrier oil (one teaspoon)

Mix all of this together under the light of a yellow candle a day before you start the work. Leave it overnight and your oil is ready.

What You Will Need

- Yellow candle
- Piece of paper
- Clarity Oil
- Pen

The Work

1. Write down on the piece of paper one goal that you want to achieve for your business. Be very specific. Statements like "I want to be rich" are not helpful. Instead, try something like, "I want to develop a profitable business idea."
2. Add a few drops of Clarity Oil to the paper.
3. Position the candle at the center of your ancestor altar and light it.
4. Place the goal paper in front of the candle with the goal facing up.
5. Fold down the top third of the paper, and the bottom third of the paper up.
6. Fold the left third of the paper to the right, and the right third of the paper to the left. You've created a simple envelope.
7. When the candle has burned for a bit, drop nine drops of wax onto your envelope to seal it closed.
8. When you are done, express your gratitude to the spirits and then put out the candle.

Carry the paper with you at all times until you have achieved the goal.

DRAW MONEY WITH BASIL

The color green symbolizes wealth, abundance, and prosperity. The green in basil is the perfect shade for a rootwork that is designed to attract money, which is why basil is used often in Hoodoo for money and prosperity work. Also, the rich scent plays a very important role in fulfilling all your intentions for this spell. It leads the money spirits to your door and keeps your path to financial success clear.

For this spell, we are going to combine strong elements linked to money spirits and put them in a location that will act as a beacon for money. These funds that you are expecting can come through business transactions, generous friends or luck in your financial endeavors. You must feed it consistently to keep its power strong.

This work also uses high john root, an incredibly important root in Hoodoo. Explaining high john requires its own section, but for now, know that it brings success through cunning and luck. Honestly, carrying a high john root in your pocket is probably the simplest Hoodoo you can do to bring success and luck into your life.

What You Will Need:

- Green thread
- Basil
- High john root
- Piece of paper
- Pen
- Money Drawing Oil

The Work

1. Write down your name and birthdate three times on the paper on three separate lines.
2. Place the high john root in the basil and wrap it. Ensure that you have enough basil to cover up the root.
3. Use the name paper to wrap the basil.
4. Dip the thread in the Money Drawing Oil.
5. Wrap the thread around the name paper to secure it.
6. Tie three knots in the thread, and leave a little extension so you can use it to hang the conjure.
7. Hang this work over the entrance door of your home or business.
8. Every day, rotate it in a circle and speak your intentions. You can say something like, "Money, I command you to come to me. I command abundant wealth to come to my business."

Feed this ball every day with the three drops of Money Drawing Oil. You can also pray Psalm 23 every time you feed it. Focus on the part that says, "I shall not lack."

PROTECT YOUR MONEY WITH THE ROSE OF JERICHO

Sometimes it isn't about drawing money to you, but keeping what you have. I've certainly been in the position where money seems to be flowing out of my pocketbook faster than it goes in. Now, sometimes that's a person's own fault for spending money on frivolous things.

But sometimes unexpected costs pop up - a car breaks down, your child needs a doctor's visit, your landlord increases your rent.

To help protect your finances, you can use the wonderful Rose of Jericho. This amazing plant looks like a tumbleweed from an old cowboy movie, all shrunken and curled up. It appears quite dead. But add a bit of water to it and it unfolds and turns a dark green: the color of abundance. That's why it's also known as the resurrection plant. When it dries out, it curls back up and can hold onto something, like a closed fist. That makes it special in Hoodoo for protection, though it can also be used in crossing work.

What You Will Need

- A Rose of Jericho
- Ancestor money - any denomination
- A piece of paper
- A white tea candle
- A small bowl of water

The Work

1. Write down what you want protected on the piece of paper. In this case, you can write "Protect my money." If you need something more specific, write it down.
2. Place the Rose of Jericho into the bowl of water. It should be submerged about halfway.
3. Wait for it to open, usually in a few hours.

4. Place the petition paper and the ancestor money into the open Rose.
5. On your ancestor altar, light the candle, and place the Rose.
6. Ask your ancestors for help protecting your money.
7. Let the candle burn out.

The Rose of Jericho will slowly close as it dries out, holding tight to your money.

SWEETEN MY BUSINESS WITH HONEYCOMB

Rootworks that are created with the intention of sweetening are designed to establish stability. When used in a relationship, it means you want your partner to be more reliable and more committed. When used in a conjure work for business, you want to create financial stability that will guarantee a steady flow of income.

Honeycombs in Hoodoo work represent stability. If you look at a honeycomb, it's a pattern that repeats and repeats, designed by nature over millions of years to be efficient and stable. And of course, it's covered with honey, which is both sweet (to draw) and sticky (to keep that money stuck to you). Now, honey is a slow sweetener, but that's fine for a long-term working. Honeycomb aids in building and positioning you for success. So, when you use a honeycomb to do your rootwork, you are building a solid foundation that will ensure your business is not a one-hit wonder. Instead, it grows, thrives and expands, all the while keeping you financially happy. It is a simple rootwork with a long-lasting impact.

What You Will Need

- A small piece of honeycomb (to sweeten and stabilize)
- Lodestone (to attract)
- Three basil leaves (to draw money)
- Piece of green cloth
- String or twine

The Work

1. Place the green cloth at the center of your altar.
2. Put the honeycomb at the center of the green cloth.
3. Put the lodestone and basil leaves on top of the honeycomb.
4. Wrap the green cloth to cover everything and tie it closed.
5. Bury the bundle close to your business or home.

This spell can also be used if you are uncertain about your job. Repeat the process mentioned here, but in the last step, bury it close to your place of work.

PROTECT YOUR BUSINESS MOJO BAG WITH DEVIL'S CLAW

The Devil's Claw is an herb with a very strong protective energy. Despite its name, it doesn't have any diabolical properties. It draws its name from the claw-like shape of its seed pods, which are long and hooked.

While the Rose of Jericho is good for general protection, I find Devil's Claw more useful when you need protection from something specific. Think of the Rose of Jericho like a shield protecting you, while Devil's Claw is more like a sword swiping at any who would harm you. For a business, that could be something like losing employees, preventing theft, or keeping customers coming back.

What You Will Need:

- Devil's Claw root, dried or powdered - one tablespoon
- Dried five finger grass - to ward off evil - one teaspoon
- Goldenseal root - for protection - one teaspoon
- Money Drawing Oil
- Piece of paper
- Pen
- Green cloth
- Twine

The Work

1. On the piece of paper, write down your business's name along with your intention. Something like, "Stop people from stealing from me."
2. Pour 7 drops of Money Drawing Oil on the paper.
3. Put the herbs on top of the petition paper and fold it closed as best you can.
4. Wrap the paper with the green cloth.
5. Secure the green cloth with a twine.
6. Put it in a safe location in your business.

A mojo bag is a small spirit, and must be fed. You should feed the mojo bag regularly with either rum, Hoyt's Cologne, or holy water. A few drops once per week should do. Each time you feed it, remind the spirit inside what you want it to do.

REPUTATION SAVER MOJO BAG WITH SUNFLOWER SEEDS

In a career or business, your reputation is everything. A single piece of gossip can burn down all you have worked hard for. To prevent that from happening, you need a binding spell that will shut the mouths of anyone who speaks ill of your reputation. Another way this work comes in handy is to help socially awkward people from saying things that could land them in trouble.

If you are the type of person who speaks inappropriately when you are forced into the spotlight, a binding spell like this will ensure that you don't say anything that will damage your integrity. I would recommend using this conjure work right before you give a presentation. This will help you focus on what you have put together for potential clients and remove or shut out anything you might say that could backfire negatively.

The key ingredient for this work is sunflower seeds. The sunflower represents light and integrity, and using it in this conjure work will help you to project yourself or your business in a positive light that other people will find appealing. In doing so, your reputation will be kept intact.

What You Will Need

- Sunflower seeds - one tablespoon
- Rosemary essential oil - to protect - three drops
- Chia seeds - to stop gossip - one tablespoon
- Crossroads dirt - to carry off any bad things that people think about you - one tablespoon
- A piece of paper
- Pen
- Silver coin (or substitute three pennies)
- Cloth bag
- Twine

The Work

1. Write down your name and birthdate three times on three different lines on the paper.
2. Put three drops of rosemary oil on the paper.
3. Place the sunflower seeds, dirt from a crossroads, and silver coin in the paper.
4. Fold up the paper, and say this nine times: "Let no one speak ill of me."
5. Place the paper into the cloth bag and tie it closed with the twine.

Take this bag with you whenever you go to work, or before you give a presentation. If you are going to be pitching your services to a client, you can have this bag in your pocket while you do so, especially if you are worried about saying the wrong things.

SEAL THE DEAL WITH PANCAKE SYRUP

Are you trying to make a sale? Have you just concluded an interview with a hiring manager and you want to seal the deal on that job? Are you still in the process of negotiating your salary in the new firm where you are hoping to work? What you need is a Hoodoo work that will seal the deal for you, and we are going to do that with pancake syrup.

Pancake syrup is a good sweetener, and it's sticky like honey, making it good for sealing a deal. I find it works faster than honey, but the effects don't last as long. So it's good for when you want something to stick, and stick soon, but don't need it to last a long time. For example, if you are going to sell something to a client and it is a one-off deal, a pancake syrup can deliver that to you.

If you are negotiating your salary with the HR person and you are sure that you will not be working with them in the future, this is also what you want to use. Do this before you conclude that deal and everything will move in your favor.

What You Will Need

- Pancake syrup
- Jar
- Brown paper
- Pen

The Work

1. Write down the name of the person you want to seal the deal with on the piece of paper three times.
2. Put the syrup in a pan and leave it to boil. Syrup may be faster than honey, but boiling it will speed it up.
3. When it is bubbling, pour the syrup into a jar.
4. Put the person's name paper in the jar.
5. Store in a dark place and then go ahead with the deal.
6. Dispose of the jar in running water as soon as the deal is done.

To give more power to the spell, you can substitute something personal from the target instead of using a name paper. Things like pieces of their clothing, their handwritten signature, and so on would work just fine. Just swap out their name paper and follow the rest of the instructions.

GET A PROMOTION MOJO BAG WITH MUD DAUBER NEST

Mud daubers are a type of wasp that build their nests out of mud. You can often find their nests on the side of houses or trees, where they make little columns protected from the rain. I'm not a fan of wasps, but I do respect mud daubers. Carrying that mud from the ground up to where they want to build is no small feat for such a tiny creature!

In Hoodoo, we use their nests when we want to inspire diligence and hard work, which is what you'll need if you want a promotion. This work isn't for your boss, it's for you. It will make you into such a good worker that your boss will have no choice but to promote you! Of course, you can also give the mojo bag to someone else who may need a boost.

In addition to the mud dauber nest, we are going to work with gravel roots and calendula. Gravel roots are for attracting jobs, so when you put this inside of a petition, it binds your petition to the thing that you desire. Calendula, on the other hand, is good for luck. So, let us get to work.

What You Will Need

- Mud dauber nest powder - three teaspoons
- Gravel root powder - one teaspoon
- Calendula powder - one teaspoon
- Dried Peppermint leaves - five leaves
- Green thread
- Green cloth bag
- Twine or string
- Pen
- A piece of paper

The Work

1. Write down your name and birthdate three times on three different lines on the piece of paper.
2. Put all the herbs and mud dauber nest powder on the name paper.

3. Spray with the Favor Cologne from a few spells back.
4. Wrap the paper around the herbs and put it all into the cloth bag.
5. Tie the bag shut with the twine or string.
6. Spray the mojo bag with the Favor Cologne again.
7. Place overnight on your ancestor altar and petition your ancestors for the job you want. Be realistic but don't be afraid to go for what you really want.

Put the packet in your pocket and take it everywhere with you until the job you petitioned manifests. When that happens, you can gently discard it or bury it. Until then, spray it once a week with Favor Cologne.

BANISH A TROUBLESOME COLLEAGUE WITH PEPPERS

For this work, we are trying to get rid of that annoying colleague who gets on your last nerve. I know that sometimes we meet people with whom we have disagreements every other day. This is normal, as long as neither of you feels disrespected. But once in a blue moon you come across that person who simply takes delight in running you down. They seem to have made it their life's mission to torment you. For this work, we are looking at that nasty colleague but it can also be used for relatives, neighbors, or anyone else you encounter who causes problems for you.

This is a variant of hot foot powder, which causes irritation to the target when they cross over it. There are many ways to make hot foot powder, and you can vary the ingredients to change the effects. For instance, the hotter the peppers used, the more irritation the person will feel. You can use banana peppers for a mild effect, or jalapeno for a quicker and more dramatic result. Be careful which you choose. At work, a slower, more subdued affect may be better than a quick, dramatic one.

What You Will Need

- Dried hot peppers (your choice) - one tablespoon
- Black pepper (for extra irritation) - three teaspoons
- Mustard seeds (to cause confusion) - three teaspoons
- Dirt from a busy road (to compel them to leave) - three teaspoons
- Yellow candle
- A pot with a handle
- A jar
- A fire or stove

The Work

1. Light the candle.
2. Mix all the ingredients together in the pot.
3. Speak your intentions in a clear and concise way. Say something like, "Our path will now be separated. You will go your way and leave me be."
4. Hold the mixture in the bowl above the flame. Turn it around counter-clockwise as you say the words.
5. Put the pot above the fire or on the stove. When it feels hot,

remove it to cool. You only need it to become hot to the touch.

6. Take the mix with you and sprinkle it inside your colleague's shoes, or on a road that you know they will walk on, or else at their seat at work.

This spell is not intended to bring harm or calamity to the target. It simply removes them from the immediate environment where they cause conflict for you.

BOSS FIX PACKET WITH TOBACCO

I'm sure we can all agree that life is easier when we have the favor of the boss. Many times, people go to extremes to get the boss's attention, in the hopes of securing their favor. You don't need to go down that route and stoop beneath your station in the process. With this work, you can fix it so that you become your boss's favorite person.

Tobacco leaves, which are the focus of this conjure, have many uses in Hoodoo, stemming from African slaves' knowledge of it from working on the plantation. It is most often used for protection or domination. In this case, you want to dominate your boss, but not in a way that makes it obvious to everyone that you are in control. You want to be the one who they favor above all others.

You can get the tobacco for this work by cutting open a cigarette. Also, if you are a woman with a boss who is harassing you for sexual favors, adding a few drops of your menstrual blood in the work will stop the harassment, and greatly increase the power of the spell.

However, that's only effective if your boss has a sexual interest in you.

What You Will Need

- Tobacco - one cigarette's worth
- Calamus root - for domination - one teaspoon
- A piece of paper
- Pen
- Black cotton string
- Black cloth bag
- Favor Cologne

The Work

1. Write down your boss's name and birthdate three times on the paper. If you don't know the birthdate, you can skip that part.
2. Spray a few drops of the Favor Cologne on the name paper.
3. Put the calamus root and tobacco in the name paper.
4. Put the bundle into the black cloth bag.
5. Tie the bag closed with the black cotton string.
6. Tie nine knots when you are done. (If you are a woman trying to control your boss, put one drop of your menstrual blood on each knot).
7. Call your boss's name nine times and tell him/her to freely give you whatever you want.
8. Place the packet in the space where your boss works.

You can enhance the work by reciting Genesis 39:2-4 during the preparation of the conjure.

RESTORE PASSION FOR YOUR WORK BATH WITH SAFFRON

Saffron is an herb that infuses passion into whatever you are using it for. When you work at a job, the general expectation is that every few years you will advance to the next stage in terms of skills, your position, and your financial compensation. However, many people find themselves stagnating in their jobs.

They spend longer than they should in the same spot. In time, whatever passion they have for their job fizzles out, leaving them both mentally and physically stuck. With this particular Hoodoo work, you can activate genuine passion in a job situation. Patchouli promotes wealth and progress, while gravel root is focused on bringing blessings to your job.

So with these three herbs working together, you are immersing yourself in a situation in which your passion for your work is reignited and then blessings over that job are activated. With all of these elements in play, you are strategically positioned to stand out to your superiors, and they see you as a prime candidate for promotion.

What You Will Need

- Saffron - one cup
- Patchouli (to move forward) - one cup
- Gravel root (to bring blessings) – one cup

- A pot of water
- A stove
- Spray bottle
- A strainer

The Work

1. Pour the ingredients into the pot.
2. Bring the water to a boil.
3. Let half the water boil away, then set the pot aside to cool.
4. Strain into a spray bottle and dispose of the herbs in running water.
5. In a bathtub or shower, wash the water over yourself. Take your time, and think of the parts of your work that you actually like, or liked when you first started.

You can enhance the bath by reciting Psalm 23 while you wash. Before leaving for work, spray on some of the Favor Cologne to help bring you good fortune.

LANDLORD FIX WITH PEANUT BUTTER

As renters, the joy you experience at home depends on the relationship you have with your landlord. If your landlord is only interested in collecting the rent, you could end up with numerous situations where broken items and fixtures around the house are abandoned, leaving you somewhat handicapped.

Then if you want changes, the costs have to come out of your own pocket. You can fix that situation by preparing this work with peanut butter. I enjoy most Hoodoo works that involve peanut butter. Peanut is a powerful restrictive element. It is particularly useful if you have lost a relationship, money, or a job.

A good conjure work that involves peanut butter can restore these for you. In this context, we are trying to restore balance to the relationship that you have with the landlord because your landlord is not only there to collect rent. They are supposed to maintain the home so that your stay there remains comfortable.

What You Will Need

- Peanut butter
- Three pieces of paper
- Pen
- Twine

The Work

1. On the first paper, write down your address.
2. On the second paper, write down the name of your landlord.
3. On the third paper, write down the task you want them to carry out. The instructions must be short and clear.
4. Take a little bit of the peanut butter and rub it on the landlord's name paper.
5. Stick the address paper on top of it.

6. Rub a little bit of peanut butter on the address paper and stick the instruction paper on top of it.
7. Roll all three papers to form a cylindrical shape.
8. Tie it up with twine.
9. Hang it in front of your house. Your landlord will do as the instruction paper commands.

You must be clear on what you want them to do. Your instruction on the paper should be short and straight to the point. Something like, "fix the plumbing" or "don't be mad at a late payment" would work.

DREAM HOME PURCHASE WITH SHOES

The ability to buy the home of your dreams is a luxury that not many can afford. And even those who have worked hard enough to raise the funds to afford this dream could find themselves in a market that is currently inflated, making it almost impossible to achieve this goal. But with a little help from your ancestors, all the elements you need to manifest your dreams can be brought together in your favor.

This conjure will help the owners of the property favor your bid above all others, so you'll have to have a specific house in mind first. The offer you make for the house will be appealing to the seller and any circumstance or roadblock that will hinder the process will be eliminated.

Hoodoo uses foot tracks and shoes in a lot of workings. This type of magic comes directly from Africa, where our ancestors knew tracks were connected to the animals and people who made them. Sometimes foot track magic works by crossing a person's path with a working like hot foot powder, so that when they cross the powder, the spell takes effect. Hoodoo also works with shoes as representing both a person's tracks and as a personal item attached to them.

What You Will Need

- One green candle
- One yellow candle
- Two pieces of paper
- Pen
- Favor Cologne
- A pair of shoes (yours)

The Work

1. Write down the address of your dream home on each of the pieces of paper.
2. Dress the papers with the Favor Cologne.
3. Insert each of the pieces of paper in each shoe.
4. Walk around the building you want to buy nine times, then return home.
5. Remove the paper from each shoe and set it aside.
6. Light both candles at your altar.
7. Burn the papers in the flames of these candles, one piece of paper per candle.
8. After you've finished, dispose of the tools for the spell in running water.

Please note that this spell is meant to be carried out before you place the bid on the house. You can put the papers into your shoes before doing a walk-through, and then walk around the house nine times as part of that process.

THE GAMBLER'S CHARM WITH IRON PYRITE

Wherever anyone used to go in the world, throughout history, if they had gold, they were rich. The allure of gold drove the Spanish and Portuguese to explore the New World, and to exploit it they began importing slaves from Africa. Those slaves, separated from everything they knew, did everything they could to hold on to their spiritual traditions. Eventually, those traditions, mixed with what they learned in the New World, grew into Hoodoo.

The African slaves, of course, never got any of that gold. But they did occasionally come across iron pyrite, also called fool's gold. Iron pyrite has nearly the same luster as gold, and our ancestors realized that luster was wonderful for drawing abundance. And iron pyrite has a quality that makes it even better than gold for Hoodoo workings - it's magnetic, just like a lodestone. That combination of looking like gold and drawing like a lodestone makes it wonderful for drawing money. When combined with bay leaves and a pair of dice, you get a very handy lucky charm for gambling.

What You Will Need

- One iron pyrite crystal
- Three fresh bay leaves (to bring success)

- A pair of dice
- White candle
- Red cloth bag
- String or twine
- Van Van oil (for good luck)

The Work

1. Light the candle.
2. Place the iron pyrite crystal, bay leaves, and dice into the cloth bag.
3. Tie it closed with the string or twine.
4. Feed it nine drops of Van Van oil.
5. Tell the spirit inside what you want to do. Something like, "Help me roll the dice well" would do.

Carry this mojo bag with you before gambling to improve your odds. You should feed it Van Van oil before each time you gamble, or at least once a week to keep the spirit inside alive and happy.

ST. JUDE FOR A MIRACLE

The saints play a very important role in Hoodoo conjure. When the African slaves arrived in the New World and were forced to adopt Christianity, they recognized many of the saints as manifestations of the same spirits they venerated in their homeland. Over time, Hoodoo incorporated beseeching the saints for aid as a powerful way to help a conjure. Now, I want to note that not all Hoodoo workers work with saints, since many Hoodoo workers come from predominantly Protestant areas and Protestants don't venerate the saints as Catholics do. But, as I've tried to make clear, there is no one "right" way to practice Hoodoo, and it varies from one place to the next. Louisiana, where my people are from, was predominantly Catholic back then, so we incorporated those elements into our Hoodoo. A similar thing happened with Voodoo, but that's a whole other book's worth of discussion.

Different saints are called on for different needs. Saint Jude, for instance, is the patron saint of lost causes. At a point in your life where faith is hanging in the balance and you are unsure of what the next moment will bring, a miracle might be the only thing that can pull you back from the edge of destruction.

There are different types of miracles that you can request from Saint Jude. But for the purpose of this conjure, our focus is going to be on finance. If you are desperately in need of financial favor... and I'm talking about the kind of financial favor that only a miracle can deliver to you, this is the conjure for you.

You should always give an offering when working with a saint. For Saint Jude, water and bread are appropriate.

What You Will Need:

- Statue or picture of St. Jude
- Piece of paper
- Cup of water
- Bread (any type will do)

- White candle

The Work

1. Place the statue or picture of Saint Jude on your altar.
2. Place the bread and water on your altar as an offering to St Jude.
3. Light the candle.
4. Ask Saint Jude for help. Speak from your heart and tell him what you need.

After the candle has gone out, leave the bread and water overnight. The next day you can remove the bread from your altar and dispose of it in your trash without worry. St. Jude will already have received your offering by then.

This work may seem like a simple prayer, but remember that you're doing it on your ancestor altar. That way it's not just you asking, it's all your ancestors crying out on your behalf!

CONCLUSION

There are no words to describe the feeling you get when you successfully complete a spell. To know that you can reach into the spiritual world and get help feels like such an incredible relief - you know that you're not alone. Your ancestors are out there, and they want to help you.

However, your first few workings may not turn out the way you intended. Hoodoo is a skill, and like any skill, it takes time to become good at it. You can't get off a couch and run a marathon without a lot of practice, and you can't master the spiritual world the first time you approach your ancestor altar. You will become better with practice, I promise. When I was a young girl just getting started, I was a mess. But my grandmother, Mama Estelle, encouraged me to keep going. I want you to do the same.

Also remember that some spells take time. Expecting to get an immediate result after you carry out a conjure is not realistic. Some spells work very fast, but most of them require at least a few days' interval in order to be effective.

Give it time to marinate and get going. For the most part, you are working with the help of the spirits. Your first foray into Hoodoo work is an introduction to your ancestors. They will be interested in working with you, but you have to establish a relationship with them. This is why I always recommend putting offerings on your altar. Coffee, rum, and even sweets are little gifts that the spirits of our ancestors often enjoy.

Think of it this way: when you want to ask someone for a favor, you don't just walk up to a complete stranger and recite your list of petitions to them. Your first instinct is to try to establish some kind of relationship with them so they are more inclined to listen to you and then respond. It is the same way with spirits. Get to know them. And don't worry, it won't take long for spirits to warm up to you, especially if they are your ancestral spirits.

If anything, they will be delighted to have the opportunity to be involved in the affairs of your life. Enjoy the opportunities that conjure brings your way. Embrace your roots and your identity by connecting with your ancestors. This connection will empower your spells and turn you into a powerful Hoodoo worker in no time. Most importantly, enjoy yourself. Learn. Grow. Evolve.

It is my fervent hope and desire that your dreams and aspirations will come true and that you live a life that brings you genuine happiness and contentment.

Made in the USA
Columbia, SC
28 July 2022